C QUARTE
LEEDS METROPOL

INTRODUCTION
TO
PUBLIC
RELATIONS

INTRODUCTION TO PUBLIC RELATIONS

SAM BLACK, MBE, FIPR, FBIM, MJI, FBCO, FRSA

Honorary Professor of Public Relations
University of Stirling

Visiting Professor of Public Relations
College of St Mark and St John Plymouth

Foreword by Dr Edward L Bernays

Introduction by Rita Bhimani,
Chairman, IPRA Education and Research Committee

International
Public Relations
Association

The Modino Press Limited

To GWEN for her constructive criticism and unfailing encouragement

First published July 1989

Published by
The Modino Press Limited
Keswick House, 3 Greenway
London N20 8EE

in conjunction with the
International Public Relations Association

© Sam Black 1989

ISBN 0 903629 03 8

Text set in 10/12 English Times
Printed in Great Britain and distributed by
Roman Press Limited, 19 Woodside Road, Bournemouth BH5 2BA

Contents

PART II   METHODS OF PUBLIC RELATIONS

PART III   PUBLIC RELATIONS IN ACTION

APPENDIXES

Introduction
by Rita Bhimani, Chairman,
IPRA Education and Research
Committee

IPRA welcomes this new book by IPRA Past President Sam Black as it should contribute to a wider understanding of the theory and practice of public relations. It is part of IPRA's commitment to the encouragement of professional practice and the highest possible standards of performance that rely on a comprehensive body of knowledge and bibliographical resources.

Two features of the book are worthy of special notice. The 'wheel of education' developed from discussions at the series of educators' meetings, initiated by IPRA in September 1980, which led to the publication of IPRA Gold Paper No 4, 'A Model for Public Relations Education for Professional Practice' which has had such a profound influence on the development of public relations education in many countries.

The second feature which I commend is the author's emphasis on professional standards and codes of conduct. The text explains the importance of ethical behaviour at all times and the appendix gives the full text of IPRA codes and similar codes.

Public relations is an integral function of good management but can only make its full contribution if practitioners have a comprehensive base of knowledge and resources. In supporting this book, to be followed by others, IPRA is making a positive effort to improve the availability of definitive public relations texts.

July 1989   Calcutta

Foreword
by Dr Edward Bernays

The name of Sam Black is synonymous with in-depth understanding of the profession of public relations, an art applied to a science in which the primary consideration is the public interest.

During four years as Secretary General of the International Public Relations Association, Sam Black secured world-wide recognition of public relations as a profession concerned with advice on action to bring about adjustment between organisations and their publics.

It is a tribute to Sam Black and his competence that this book is the successor to 'Practical Public Relations', first published in 1962. Its regular reprint spanning twenty-five years attests to its continuing valuable contribution to the field it encompasses. This is an accolade to the author which will, I am sure, be enhanced by the value of this new text.

Public relations today, according to the attestation of leaders in profit and non-profit fields alike, commands an increasingly important place in policy-making strategies and action programmes.

The comprehensive scope of the book should encourage a greater conformity in practice in the profession world-wide. The phrase 'public relations' is today in the public domain and anybody can use it to mean almost anything. Words today have the stability and permanence of soap bubbles. This book should develop a better understanding of the true nature of public relations, how it can be effectively practised, and what it can accomplish in this complex world.

Maladjustments between individuals and groups of all kinds disturb the progress of society. The function of the public relations professional is to promote harmony and mutual understanding. This book outlines how the profession applies the findings of the social sciences to the adjustments of everyday life and should be a valuable textbook for students of public relations and all concerned with management.

July 1989   Edward L Bernays, BS, DH(Hon), LLD(Hon)

Preface

Public relations has become generally accepted as an important element of business, government and all aspects of everyday life. *Accepted* does not necessarily mean understood. This new book explains the parameters of public relations practice and the valuable part it can play in extending the frontiers of good management, caring government and peaceful coexistence in the interdependent world in which we all live.

This text is the natural successor to my first book *Practical Public Relations* which has passed through many editions and has been translated into several different languages. One hears that it has introduced many into the profession and has done much to encourage an accurate picture of the art and science of public relations.

With the continuing expansion of public relations degree programmes in Britain and many other countries, there is a need for a definitive book which explains in detail the basic theory and practice of the subject and covers the new concern with issues management, social responsibility, crisis public relations, lobbying and other factors which have become of greater significance as public relations practice reaches 65 years of service to the common weal in most of the developed and developing countries of the world.

There is no mystique in public relations. It is an integral part of the effective management of any organised activity but requires training and experience, commonsense and application.

Through continuing involvement in the International Public Relations Association, one realises the universal application of public relations to almost every country, both in the public and private sector. It has been my privilege to meet colleagues in many countries and to note their increasing contribution to their national welfare.

Acknowledgment is due to many who have shared with me the excitement and scenarios of working together in a field that is always challenging but very rewarding. In particular, to my late wife, Muriel, my partner for so many years.

July 1989   SAM BLACK

Part 1

Defining the Subject—
Theory and Practice

1 Public Relations Today

The purpose of public relations practice is to establish two-way communication seeking common ground or areas of mutual interest, and to establish understanding based on truth, knowledge and full information.

The scale of activity to promote good public relations may vary considerably according to the size and nature of the interested parties, but the philosophy, the strategy and the methods will be very similar whether the public relations programme is designed to influence international understanding or to improve relations between a company and its customers, agents and employees.

In a family, or a small, closely-knit community, there are few obstacles to mutual discussion and the communication of ideas, but even here there is plenty of opportunity for misunderstanding. In public or commercial life, however, the 'family' circle is usually widely dispersed and the absence of personal contact makes cooperation and understanding more difficult. People skilled in public relations practice use modern methods of communication and persuasion to bridge the gap to establish mutual understanding.

Understanding is conditioned by reputation, previous experience and cultural factors. To cultivate a good reputation, a credible identity and a positive corporate strategy are an important integral part of most public relations programmes.

THE WORLD OF PUBLIC RELATIONS

The term 'public relations' is widely used these days, but often in the wrong context. The full breadth of public relations practice covers ten separate groups:

1 Public Opinion.
2 Public Affairs.
3 Government Relations.
4 Community Affairs.
5 Industrial Relations.
6 Financial Affairs.
7 International Relations.
8 Consumer Affairs.
9 Research and Statistics.
10 Media of Communication.

These are the main fields in which public relations practice plays an important part, and while the theory and philosophy of public relations as explained in this book applies equally to all these different fields, naturally the details and the priorities will be different.

Public relations can make an important contribution to good management in the widest sense of the word. The following list gives the many different avenues in which the professional public relations man or woman may work:

1 Counselling based on an understanding of human behaviour.

2 Analysing future trends and predicting their consequences.

3 Research into public opinion, attitudes and expectations and advising on necessary action.

4 Establishing and maintaining two-way communication based on truth and full information.

5 Preventing conflict and misunderstandings.

6 Promoting mutual respect and social responsibility.

7 Harmonising the private and the public interest.

8   Promoting good-will with staff, suppliers and customers.

9   Improving industrial relations.

10 Attracting good personnel and reducing labour turnover.

11 Promotion of products or services.

12 Maximising profitability.

13 Projecting a corporate identity.

To achieve success, all public relations activity must be based on truth and full information and be carried out on a continuing basis. It can never be a substitute for good performance, and indeed it is likely to expose any intrinsic weaknesses. Correct timing is very important, and the establishment of priorities is essential at an early stage of planning.

A typical public relations activity will have four separate but related parts:

1   Analysis, research and defining problems.

2   Drawing up a programme of action and budget.

3   Communicating and implementing the programme.

4   Monitoring the results, evaluation and possible modification.

This is sometimes referred to as the RACE system: Research, Action, Communication and Evaluation.

DEFINITIONS

There is a danger of devoting too much emphasis on questions of definition since there have been so many different definitions of public relations practice suggested during the past sixty years. However, it is necessary to study a few definitions.

The Institute of Public Relations (IPR), which was formed in the United Kingdom in February 1948, adopted a definition of public relations practice which (slightly amended in November 1987) is still valid. The Institute's definition is 'public relations practice is the planned and sustained effort to establish and maintain goodwill and mutual understanding between an organisation and its publics'.

Of all current definitions the best is the Mexican Statement, signed by representatives of more than 30 national and regional public relations associations in Mexico City on 11 August 1978. This stated that:

Public Relations practice is the art and social science of analyzing trends, predicting their consequences, counselling organisation's leadership, and implementing planned programmes of action which will serve both the organisation's and the public interest.

Dr Rex Harlow, a veteran public relations practitioner of San Francisco, examined 472 different definitions of public relations practice and distilled them into the following working definition.

Public relations is a distinctive management function which helps establish and maintain mutual lines of communication, understanding, acceptance and cooperation between an organisation and its publics; involves the management of problems or issues; helps management to keep informed on and responsive to public opinion; defines and emphasises the responsibility of management to serve the public interest; helps management keep abreast of and effectively utilise change, serving as an early warning system to help anticipate trends; and uses research and sound and ethical communication techniques as its principal tools.

The Public Relations Society of America (PRSA) issued an official statement on public relations on 6 November 1982 from which the following extract is taken:

Public relations helps our complex, pluralistic society to reach decisions and function more effectively by contributing to mutual understanding among groups and institutions. It serves to bring private and public policies into harmony.

Public relations serves a wide variety of institutions in society such as businesses, trade unions, government agencies, voluntary associations, foundations, hospitals and educational and religious institutions. To achieve their goals, these institutions must develop effective relationships with many different audiences or publics such as employees, members, customers, local communities, shareholders and other institutions and with society at large.

The managements of institutions need to understand the attitudes and values of their publics in order to achieve institutional goals. The goals themselves are shaped by the external environment. The public relations practitioner acts as a counsellor to management, and as a mediator, helping to translate private aims into reasonable, publicly acceptable policy and action.

One usually turns to a good dictionary for a reliable definition. Not all dictionary definitions of public relations are acceptable but the standard *Webster New International Dictionary* gives 'The promotion of rapport and goodwill between a person, firm or institution and other persons, special publics, or the community at large, through the distribution of interpretative material, the development of neighbourly interchange and the assessment of public reaction.'

There are many simpler definitions but they are not comprehensive. Such as 'good performance, publicly recognised', or 'doing good and getting credit for it', or 'reconciling the private and the public interest'.

The author prefers a short but comprehensive definition:

Public relations practice is the art and science of achieving harmony with the environment through mutual understanding based on truth and full information.

Theory of Communication

Public relations philosophy puts much emphasis on the need for two-way communication. This is now fairly well accepted, but how does one achieve it?

Many forms of misunderstanding spring from lack of communication, and one of the first objectives in any public relations programme is to improve existing channels of communication and to establish new ways of setting up a two-way flow of information and understanding. Even when there is a definite will to communicate, there may be great difficulty in achieving success, for the mechanisms of communication are very complicated.

Many of the difficulties in industry are ascribed to lack of communication, and managements are constantly exhorted to give information more readily and more regularly to employees and the public. Public relations methods can do much to achieve this, but let nobody underestimate the difficulties involved.

In a medium or large company there is a definite and closely related chain of communication from top management downwards, and success in communicating clearly and quickly is essential to the efficiency of the company. Research has, however, revealed some discouraging facts about this important aspect of business.

It appears that a managing director should expect his deputy to understand only 60 per cent of what he is trying to communicate to him on some important but complicated subject. In turn, the deputy will only achieve 60 per cent understanding when he passes the information on to his deputy, and so on down the line of command. So if there are five levels in an organisation, the junior manager may understand 13 per cent of the original message. This relates to the spoken message, but the results from written communication may be even worse. The understanding of a written message may be as low as 15 per cent at each level.

There was one encouraging feature of this research. When several different channels of communication are used together, the total result is much greater than the sum of the individual parts. This supports the findings of experienced public relations practitioners, who know that the best results in a public relations programme usually come from tackling a particular problem in a number of different ways at the same time.

This emphasises the benefit of supporting lectures, presentations or other forms of verbal communication by videos, slides or overhead projected illustration.

Black's Laws for Communicating Effectively
The theory of communicating in such a way that the message will be clearly understood and acted upon is almost a science in itself, but it is a question which should always be in the forefront of the public relations practitioner's mind.

I would like to suggest nine rules for communicating effectively:

1 Always insist on truth and full information.

2 Keep the message simple and straightforward.

3 Do not oversell or exaggerate.

4 Remember that half your audience are women.

5 Look for drama—do not make the communication unnecessarily drab and commonplace.

6 Package the communication appropriately—do not overdress or make it too extravagant.

7 Always take time to listen to public opinion.

8 Remember the vital importance of continuity.

9 Try to be positive and constructive in every aspect of communication.

Public Relations and Propaganda

A clear distinction must be drawn between public relations and propaganda. Goebbels described propaganda as 'an instrument of politics, a power for social control . . . . The function of propaganda is not essentially to convert; rather its function is to attract followers and to keep them in line . . . . The task of propaganda, given suitable avenues, is to blanket every area of human activity so that the environment of the individual is changed to absorb the [Nazi] movement's world view.' These quotations from Goebbels stress the great difference in the two approaches. Propaganda does not necessarily call for an ethical content, and the word is used these days mainly to describe those types of persuasion which are based solely on self-interest and in which it may be necessary to distort the facts or even to falsify them in order to achieve the purpose. Public relations, on the other hand, recognises a long-term responsibility and seeks to persuade and to achieve mutual understanding by securing the willing acceptance of attitudes and ideas. It can succeed only when the basic policy is ethical and the means used are truthful. In public relations the ends can never justify the use of false, harmful or questionable means.

It is not possible to use public relations techniques to bolster up a weak case; in fact, a successful public relations campaign may only expose the weakness. For this reason it is often stressed that good public relations must start at home. The policy should always be positive and constructive. Besides always being ethical, public relations must never be negative. Denials do not convince doubting listeners; a practical and positive demonstration of the facts is more likely to secure belief and constructive cooperation.

This important aspect of our work is dealt with comprehensively in *IPRA Gold Paper No 6*, 'Public Relations and Propaganda—values compared' by Tim Traverse-Healy (April 1988). On page 11, Professor Anne van der Meiden of Utrecht University makes the following important distinction.

'The objective of public relations is achievement of consent; of propaganda to build a movement. The intention of public relations is to achieve true dialogue; not so with propaganda. The methods of public relations involve complete openness; propaganda if needs be obscures the facts. Public relations strives for understanding; propaganda for a following.'

Identifying Publics

Under modern conditions, no government, industry, company or organisation of any kind can operate successfully without the cooperation of its publics. These publics may be both at home and overseas, but mutual understanding will be a potent factor for success in every case. Sometimes there will be overlapping; an employee may also be a shareholder and a customer.

Democracy cannot function properly without good public relations. Democracy has been defined as government of the people, by the people, for the people. The electorate requires knowledge on how government functions, information on decisions being made in its name, and education in order to take full advantage of the facilities and services provided. There is clearly need for public relations activities to help citizens understand their privileges and responsibilities under any form of government.

The need is as great in local government as it is in central government, but while the obligation has been accepted generally by government departments and agencies, the same acceptance is not always found in local government.

Mutual understanding requires, by definition, a two-way communication. A public relations policy for an industrial company, for example, should include both inward activity and intelligence to assess the policies and behaviour of the company to see whether action is necessary to improve the company's identity and commercial image, and outward activity to inform the public about the company and its achievements.

Public opinion impinges on industry at many levels: with official bodies; contact with shareholders; relations and distributors, wholesalers, etc; reactions of buyers or consumers; and internal relations with employees. In all these fields there is need for constant endeavour to establish and maintain mutual understanding and to keep a watch for possible causes of disharmony.

The social responsibility of industry is of prime importance to the welfare of a democratic society, and while many large companies have tackled this problem energetically, others have tried to pretend that they do not share a social responsibility and that they can adequately function in society without this recognition. History has repeatedly shown this assumption to be an incorrect one which, if not corrected, will be fatal to the existence of an organisation.

Corporate Social Responsibility (CSR)
It is now generally accepted that a large company has a responsibility to the community in which it operates. The first duty is to stay strong and efficient so that it can continue to reward its shareholders and employees, while making a substantial contribution to the nation's economy and welfare.

This philosophy has been accepted by big business in the USA for many years but it is now firmly established as corporate policy in Britain and in other developed countries.

The changes in the concept of CSR in the United States have been summed up thus: the 'good citizen' and 'social leader' concepts of social responsibility current in the 1970s have been merged into a 'super citizen—leader' role from which few chief executives and their companies can or should escape.

Shell has been one of the foremost exponents of CSR in Britain and the subject has been summed up by Bob Reid, chairman and chief executive of Shell UK Ltd in the following terms: 'Social responsibility is good business and good business is socially responsible'. CSR usually falls, in practical terms, into the following categories:

1   Enterprise; supporting and developing initiatives to nurture budding entrepreneurs and to boost enterprise.

2   Education; helping to bring new horizons into the lives of young people.

3   Arts and Culture; providing assistance to a range of artistic activities and bringing communities together.

4   Environment; encouraging efforts to safeguard the environment and improve the quality of life.

IBM is another company that has devoted substantial funds and resources to demonstrating its commitment to corporate citizenship. Cynics may call it 'enlightened self interest' but it is the community at large which benefits.

In the UK, many leading companies have joined together to fund schemes to help Small Businesses and other forms of enterprise. Apart from joint schemes of this kind, most of the companies devote considerable resources to direct action in the four categories listed above. There is usually a committee which decides on the allocation of funds and the CEO prefers not to be personally involved.

Sir Hector Laing, chairman of United Biscuits, initiated the 'Percentage Club' to which many leading British companies belong. Member companies pledge to donate one per cent of profits before tax to the community.

One substantial method is helping by the 'secondment' method. The company seconds staff to help worthwhile causes. The secondees are usually young mid-term career men and women or senior executives in the last few years before retirement. British Rail had 67 secondees out in the community in 1989. This is a very substantial CSR effort as the salaries amount to £900,000 per year and this is met by British Rail.

'Help in kind' is another well established avenue of assistance to the community. This takes many different forms according to the company's major activities. Some companies donate useful commodities like paint or timber, others present redundant office equipment, while others give consultancy services or the use of office or workshop accommodation.

In CSR, the company giving funds does not attempt to gain any advertising benefit or undue identification and this distinguishes CSR from sponsorship. The company is content with a 'warm glow' and the belief that social responsibility is good business.

Sponsorship, on the other hand, can be defined as 'the provision of resources to build a relationship of mutual benefit, designed to satisfy the objectives of all parties'.

Issues Management

Any organisation which does not have its head in the sand must be sensitive to future trends and awake to possible ways in which these trends may infringe on the organisation's future success. Sometimes this is called 'futurism', and another term used is 'environmental scanning', but issues management is a better term as it suggests that one does not merely monitor change but plans to take it into continuing consideration in planning corporate strategy.

To quote two sources, 'issues are unsolved problems' or 'an issue is merely a trend whose time has come'. The Conference Board of America has defined an issue as 'a condition or pressure, either internal or external, that, if it continues, will have a significant effect on the functioning of the organisation or its future interests.'

W Howard Chase has defined issues management as 'the process of identifying issues, analysing those issues, setting priorities, selecting programme strategy options, implementing a programme of action and communication, and evaluating effectiveness'. This definition appears to be an elaboration of public relations practice as defined in the Mexican Statement which is given on page 4.

Defining Objectives and Planning a Programme
The methods and skills to develop mutual understanding can be provided by public relations activity, but first it is essential to define the objectives. Only when the objectives have been defined and agreed is it possible to plan a programme. There may be both short-term and long-term objectives and in each case the timing is of prime importance. Some form of research will be necessary before any programme can be planned completely, and it will be necessary to monitor results as a campaign gathers momentum. The findings may indicate the advisability of amendment to the original plan, and it is wise to keep the campaign as flexible as possible to take into account any change of circumstances. Public relations practice is rather like playing a game of chess: 10 per cent intuition, 25 per cent experience and 65 per cent hard work.

A Dual Function
Most of the confused ideas that exist about public relations spring from the fact that it is both an advisory and an executive function. Sometimes 'public relations' is used to describe the advisory aspect, and 'publicity' the actual execution of it. It is preferable to use 'public relations' to describe the whole field, and it will be thus used in this book. Again, 'publicity' is sometimes used to describe paid-for activities such as exhibitions, films, publications, etc, while 'public relations' is reserved for actions which do not incur direct expenditure. This distinction is quite artificial and of little practical value.

Public relations is everything from an attitude of mind to a minute detail in the successful implementation of a programme. As with many activities, it is possible to pick out individual acts for criticism or ridicule, but any serious assessment of public relations must take into account its full ambit.

There is an interesting analogy between medicine and public

relations. A medical practitioner and a public relations practitioner must both first diagnose and then treat. It is common for both to be called in after the damage is done. Preventive public relations is just as important as preventive medicine and like the latter is equally rarely employed.

Codes of Professional Conduct

There are also points of similarity in training and professional behaviour in medicine and public relations. After completing lengthy and comprehensive studies, a doctor qualifies by the passing of professional examinations and is admitted to the medical register. From then on a doctor may practise as a general practitioner or take further training to become a consultant; or he may choose to work in some allied field such as research or industry. Two common factors apply to all these doctors, and indeed to all doctors of whatever nationality they may be: they all possess a minimum basic knowledge of medicine and surgery, and they subscribe to the Hippocratic oath.

A parallel exists for those engaged in public relations. All public relations practitioners—whatever their particular field of work—need to possess a basic knowledge and experience of the methods and media of the art and should subscribe to an accepted code of professional conduct.

The Institute of Public Relations has built up case law on professional conduct, and adopted a formal code in 1962. The International Public Relations Association (IPRA), has adopted a code of professional conduct, and most national public relations associations have adopted their own codes. Strict adherence to an appropriate code of professional conduct will do much to establish public relations as a profession and will help to maintain high standards. *(See* Appendix I for details of the IPRA Codes.)

IPRA, at a meeting in Athens in May 1965, adopted the International Public Relations Code of Ethics, the Code of Athens. Codes of professional conduct govern the professional behaviour of public relations practitioners in relation to people, and need therefore to be adapted to the laws, usages and customs of each country. The Code of Ethics, on the other hand, sets out the moral considerations which must be observed by all in public relations in order to preserve human values and the integrity of free communication between peoples and nations.

The European Public Relations Confederation (CERP) adopted a comprehensive code of professional conduct, the Code of Lisbon, in 1978 and amended it in 1989 *(See* Appendix I).

TRAINING AND QUALIFICATIONS

The progress made in the development of public relations education since Edward Bernays taught the first course in 1923 at New York University has been substantial. Compared to five accredited programmes in public relations in the USA in 1966, 25 universities now have accredited programmes.

Instead of offering one course in public relations, accredited institutions are providing three or more public relations courses for undergraduate majors, and graduate programmes are being strengthened.

While the USA has led the way in public relations education, other countries are now catching up fast. In Britain a full time one year programme leading to a MSc in public relations has been operating successfully since September 1988 at the University of Stirling, in Scotland and BA(Hons) degrees in public relations have been offered from September 1989 at Plymouth and Poole.

Many professionals are responding to the need for experienced professionals in the classroom and are teaching courses at nearby campuses in addition to carrying out their professional responsibilities.

The profession has also responded in providing placement opportunities for students and, to a more limited degree, fellowships and training experiences for faculty.

Research in the public relations area has increased, and the body of published material available on public relations is rapidly growing as evidenced by the PRSA bibliography printed each year.

The interdisciplinary approach to public relations education is needed for greater progress in research as well as to provide a more complete and comprehensive education at both the undergraduate and graduate levels.

Students need an understanding of psychology so that they understand motivation and persuasion; a better background in political science for the understanding of how government functions so that it can be made more responsive to societal needs; an understanding of anthropology so that they understand change and how it takes place and the importance of cultural adaptation; and of sociology so that they are able to more accurately evaluate societal trends and human interaction.

Common sense, curiosity, objectivity, logic and clear thinking are perhaps the most important assets of a successful public relations practitioner, and these cannot be taught in the classroom. Nevertheless, it is necessary to have in addition an appreciation and practical experience of public relations media, methods and techniques and these can be taught effectively if theory is supplemented by case study.

PUBLIC RELATIONS CONSULTANTS
It is regrettable that anyone can set up as a public relations consultant—and some do—without possessing the requisite knowledge and experience. These untrained newcomers to the field tend to bring the practice of public relations into disrepute. A public relations consultant should be competent to advise a client on all aspects of the subject, and should be able to advise on the employment of experts when required for specialist subjects. A wide knowledge of the world is as essential as an understanding of public relations principles and practice. The practice of public relations consultancy is discussed in some detail in the next chapter.

The present position poses difficulties to a company or organisation contemplating the appointment of a consultant. A pointer in the United Kingdom is whether or not the consultancy is a member of the Public Relations Consultants Association (PRCA) and whether the principals of the consultancy are in membership of their professional body, the Institute of Public Relations.

A consultant in other professions is a highly qualified practitioner acknowledged to be competent to give expert advice, and this should apply equally in public relations. At the moment some so-called public relations consultants are competent only to provide a press relations service and are not qualified to provide a comprehensive public relations service.

A QUESTION OF STATUS AND NOMENCLATURE
Public relations is a function of management, and public relations considerations should be taken into account when formulating policy, for subsequent public relations campaigns can never be a

satisfactory substitute for correct initial policies. It has been said, with some truth, that public relations is 90 per cent doing good and 10 per cent talking about it.

In the United States the public relations chief sometimes enjoys vice-presidential status or its equivalent, but this is not the universal practice. The deciding factor ought to be whether the qualities of the person concerned qualify him for participation in top management decisions in addition to his being responsible for coordinating and organising public relations.

It is difficult to substantiate a claim for the public relations head to be automatically a member of the top management team; the level at which he works should be settled according to the merits of each case. Whatever the level, however, it is essential that he or she should have direct and easy access to top management and preferably to the chairman or chief executive.

The failure of some companies and organisations to establish public relations as an organised part of their activities may sometimes be due to the fact that the chief executive officer considers it to be his own personal responsibility to project the personality of the concern to the outside world. Many industrial leaders regard themselves as their company's chief public relations officer and react instinctively against any suggestion that this important function should be delegated to anyone, however skilled in the art of communication.

This attitude does recognise in part the importance of public relations. The chief executive officer should set the tone for the whole organisation, but obviously he cannot spare the time to control the whole of the company's public relations activities even if he happens to possess the necessary ability and experience. In the same way that he relies on expert advice on accountancy, legal matters, architecture, sales management, etc, so does he need professional public relations advice and services.

The appropriate status that should be accorded to those engaged in public relations will depend on their responsibilities and to a certain extent on whether they are carrying out advisory or executive functions.

In a large industrial company control rests with the board of directors, and it is urged that the public relations advisers should be present at all board meetings so that they will be kept fully informed.

The senior public relations executive should also receive all agenda and minutes and thus have the opportunity of raising any relevant matters in advance. The most important factor is for the public relations officer to be involved *before* decisions are reached instead of merely receiving instructions to carry out a decision.

The public relations staff needs to understand both the agreed policy and the reasons behind the decisions to follow particular lines of action if they are to be able to interpret policy intelligently.

The question of status links up to a certain extent with problems of nomenclature. Senior practitioners use varying titles, such as director of public relations, chief information officer, public relations adviser, information officer, director of public affairs, or publicity manager. A title sometimes bears a relationship to the responsibilities involved, but in most cases it will reflect organisational arrangements and does not indicate the exact nature of the work carried out.

MEASUREMENT OF RESULTS

Much of the doubt about the value of public relations arises from the difficulties in assessing the results of public relations activities and the absence of suitable yardsticks by which these results can be measured accurately. Even where there are tangible results, as in press relations, the measurements can be misleading. Press cuttings are a tangible sign of what has appeared in the press, but if the number of column inches is to mean anything it is necessary to analyse these cuttings according to type of journal, position in the journal and its circulation and readership profile. It does not follow that because something is printed *(a)* it is read; *(b)* it is understood; or *(c)* it is favourably accepted.

Furthermore, press relations is often valuable for its success in keeping the press informed and thus avoiding rumours or mis-statements. These successes are certainly not measurable in column inches. This question reaches its acme of absurdity when sometimes the area of press cuttings is assessed at advertising rates and an attempt made to equate them to unpaid advertising. Press relations does not set itself out as, nor can it be, a substitute for advertising for there is the great difference that advertising is under the full control of the advertiser while press comment is susceptible to editorial rewriting, cutting and even complete inversion.

Certain types of campaigns would appear to lend themselves to a degree of measurement of results. For instance, if road safety public relations activities are stepped up during a period of several months, and the road casualty figures show a marked improvement in the same period, there is an assumption that the public relations campaign has been successful. There may, however, have been other factors playing an even greater part, eg weather conditions.

This simple example emphasises the difficulty of isolating the results of public relations activities. This is because public relations is an aid to management, a tool of government, and a promoter of understanding at international, national and local levels. It is rare that public relations can be isolated in its results and it is, therefore, seldom capable of accurate measurement. It has been suggested that public relations performs a somewhat similar function to that of the conductor of a symphony orchestra in bringing out the best of the individual performers and in balancing their efforts. This is a useful analogy except that public relations, unlike the efforts of the conductor, should be carried out quietly in the background wherever possible as a part of established routine management.

FACING UP TO ETHICAL PROBLEMS

Most professional men are faced from time to time with situations which present ethical problems in which there is a conflict between personal gain and the ethics of their calling.

Mention has been made of codes of professional conduct but ethics goes deeper than this. A code of conduct lays down rules for working with colleagues, relationships with journalists, and problems of this kind. More fundamental questions of ethics arise when considering such problems as whether a public relations practitioner should engage his talents to promote something that he knows or believes to be evil, or contrary to the interests of his own country. These are deep waters and the answer will often be a matter of conscience rather than logic.

The problem is likely to present itself in different forms to those working on the staff and those engaged in consultancy practice. The ethical considerations are similar, but the practical manifestations are quite distinct.

It is to be hoped that any responsible person finds out the nature of the operations of an organisation before accepting a staff

17

position. If, however, it transpires at a later date that the policy of the organisation is contrary to law or to his conscience, there can be no doubt that the public relations practitioner should resign immediately. This is an extreme example and one which does not arise often. It is more conceivable that there may be isolated actions which appear to be of somewhat doubtful honesty, or which may possibly conflict with the good of the nation or of individuals. In such circumstances it is essential to try to get these policies reversed, and if this proves unavailing then resignation must follow.

It takes courage to resign from a good position, especially if one has family responsibilities, but there can be no compromise with one's conscience under such circumstances.

To come down to more pedestrian considerations, it is very difficult to do good creative work under uncongenial conditions, and many public relations practitioners have given up comfortable and lucrative positions because they were not happy with their conditions of employment. Public relations is both a science and an art, and the best work is done by those working in a congenial atmosphere. Public relations work differs from that of, say, accountancy in that an efficient and convincing job cannot be done by an individual who has no faith in the organisation for which he is working or in its products.

Ethical problems are likely to arise in a different form for those engaged in consultancy practice. Here it is likely to be a question of whether a consultant should accept a contract to promote a cause or product which might be considered to be contrary to the public interest.

The IPRA Code of Professional Conduct expressly forbids members to have anything to do with 'front organisations'. A member must not create or make use of any organisation purporting to serve an announced cause but actually serving secret interests.

It is not necessary to be an ardent believer in a cause which you are promoting, but it is unethical to work for a cause which you believe to be wrong. For example, it would probably be generally accepted as unethical for a confirmed teetotaller to work for brewers or the wine and spirit trade.

It could perhaps be argued—to take another extreme example— that it would be wrong to do anything to publicise cigarettes, since smoking increases the likelihood of lung cancer; or to promote a wider use of butter since it may be a contributory factor in the causation of coronary thrombosis. Like ethical problems in all other walks of life, those in public relations can present great difficulty at times, but they must be faced, considered and dealt with according to conscience, for they do not lend themselves to solution by protocol.

There is bound to be a measure of special pleading in all organised public relations activities, but it is a fundamental tenet of democracy that individuals and groups shall have freedom to persuade others provided the means are fair and open. It is incumbent on all those in public relations, however, to maintain at all times a proper sense of responsibility, for their activities can influence the minds of men and have power over the progress of public affairs.

ADVERTISING AND PUBLIC RELATIONS

There is no general agreement as to the relative positions of advertising and public relations. As advertising is one of the means of communication with the public, a strong case can be made for its inclusion as a part of public relations. The fact that advertising is paid for does not affect this general point. The image that the public has of a particular company undoubtedly derives in part from the type of advertising favoured by that company.

This question is seldom faced squarely, and usually past precedent outweighs logic. The advertising department probably has deep roots, and since it spends a great deal of money it often has a director responsible for its activities. Only in a few cases does one find one person in charge of both public relations and advertising; where this does apply it works very satisfactorily. Where there are two separate departments in a large company, it is essential that close liaison should exist and it is helpful if both departments report to the same director or management committee.

An attempt is often made to distinguish between prestige or institutional advertising and advertising in support of sales activities. It is sometimes suggested that the former could come under the public relations department but never the latter. This argument is not logical, for even in an advertisement offering some article for sale the face of the firm will emerge and make an impact on public opinion. In advertising it is possible to buy space and to have control of what is said and in what form, subject to laws of decency. In public relations, however, one wishes to influence public opinion or attitudes and while we can control the message we cannot control its use.

SUMMARY

The ideas put forward in the preceding pages do not lend themselves readily to summary, but it may be helpful to list some of the things that public relations claims to be and the things that it is not.

Public relations practice includes –

1 Everything that is calculated to improve mutual understanding between an organisation and all with whom it comes into contact, both within and outside the organisation.

2 Advice on the presentation of the 'public image' of an organisation.

3 Action to discover and eliminate rumours or other sources of misunderstanding.

4 Action to broaden the sphere of influence of an organisation by appropriate publicity, advertising, exhibitions, visual aids or films.

5 Everything directed towards improving communication between people or organisations.

Public relations is NOT –

1 It is *not* a barrier between the truth and the public.

2 It is *not* propaganda to impose a point of view regardless of truth, ethics and the public interest.

3 It is *not* publicity aimed directly at achieving sales, although public relations activities are important in sales and marketing programmes.

4 It is *not* composed of stunts or gimmicks. These may be useful at times to put over ideas, but fail completely if used often or in isolation.

5 It is *not* unpaid advertising.

6 It is *not* merely press relations, although press work is a very important part of most public relations programmes.

PUBLIC RELATIONS EDUCATION

For over 50 years public relations education has been developing in universities and colleges in many countries but until recently there was little coordination. There is now a keen desire to achieve harmonisation of educational standards and a consensus has developed.

The ideal curriculum can be pictured as a series of three concentric circles. The smallest central circle encloses the subjects specifically concerned with public relations practice. The second larger circle has the subjects in the general field of communication. The third and largest circle represents the general liberal arts and humanities which are essential preparation for a successful professional.

THE WHEEL OF EDUCATION *(From the IPRA World of Public Relations Exhibition, London May 1979)*

2   The Practice of Public Relations

The theory and philosophy of public relations leads logically to a discussion of the methods by which it is practised.

Objects and Aims
The practical applications of public relations practice can be summarised under three main headings:

Positive steps to achieve goodwill
These consist in arousing and maintaining goodwill and public interest in the activities of an organisation in order to facilitate the successful operation and expansion of those activities.

Action to safeguard reputation
It is equally important to look inward at the organisation and to eliminate customs and practices which, though legitimate, are likely to offend public opinion or to interfere with mutual understanding.

Internal relationships
Using public relations techniques internally in order that the staff and employees of the organisation shall be encouraged to identify their own interests with those of the management.

These are three main avenues of public relations practice, but there are numerous connecting alleyways which make it difficult to consider the three aspects quite separately.

It is the growing interdependence of industry at home and in the international field that has contributed mainly to the remarkable spread of public relations. This is shown strikingly by the rate of increase of the membership of the Institute of Public Relations in the United Kingdom and by the formation of national public relations bodies in practically all the larger countries of the world. The Institute was founded in 1948 by a few enthusiasts, but the 1989 membership figure stands at over 3000.

The practice of public relations in Britain has developed along two main lines. Many industrial companies, trade and professional associations, and central and local government agencies, have set up public relations departments within their own organisations. Others have preferred to use the services of public relations consultants. Some use a combination of the two.

The Institute of Public Relations is a body of individuals and, therefore, includes in its membership men and women engaged in all types of public relations practice. In the early days the membership was dominated numerically by practitioners in the field of central and local government, but this balance soon altered. For some years now the majority of members has been engaged in industry. The second largest group has become those working in consultancy. There is still strong representation, however, of those working in central and local government, and for societies and associations.

At one time, many consultancies were subsidiaries of advertising agencies but experience showed that this was not satisfactory. So most consultancies in the UK, the USA and elsewhere became independent. Recently, however, some of the largest public relations consultancies have been bought by advertising agencies although they continue to operate independently.

THE CHOICE BETWEEN A STAFF OR CONSULTANCY SERVICE

It is often difficult to compare the relative merits of establishing an internal public relations organisation or of using outside consultants since there are so many varied factors involved. A discussion of these factors should help in the assessment of particular cases.

Some comments on consultancy practice have been made in Chapter 1. In general, the quality of public relations service depends on the ability and experience of those providing the service and not whether they are operating from within or outside the organisation. When a consultancy firm is employed it is necessary to consider the qualifications of the account executive actually handling the client's work.

Factors which favour the use of consultants –

1   The cost bears a direct relationship to the work commissioned, and the budget can be varied easily year by year.

2   The executives engaged on the account have worked on other types of public relations for other clients and can thus bring their wide experience to the service of each client. Moreover, the combined experience of the staff can be brought to bear on very knotty problems.

3   The principals of the consultancy are independent and can thus give unbiased and impartial advice. Outside advice is often listened to much more attentively than equally good advice from one's own staff.

4   If the results are unsatisfactory it is an easy matter to terminate the contract by giving due notice.

Practical disadvantages to weigh against these points –

1   An outside firm may have little practical knowledge of the organisation's policy or day-to-day activities, and will require detailed briefing at the outset and at every new development.

2   There may be a lack of continuity in operations, for the personnel in consultancy firms is likely to change more frequently than those in staff appointments.

3   Queries from the media which are of any complexity will usually have to be referred to someone at the headquarters of the organisation, and this hinders the provision of a speedy service.

Considerations which also favour the setting up of an internal public relations department –

1   The staff become identified with the aims and objects of the organisation and have a personal stake in its success.

2   They are able to assist the media without the constant need to refer to others.

3   Being members of the staff themselves, they are able to move freely within the organisation and to establish friendly relations at all levels. This facilitates the promotion of internal public relations activities.

4   If the size of the organisation warrants it, economy and efficiency can be increased by having specialist subsections to deal with the press, publications, photographs, etc.

The above considerations point the answer. The desirability of establishing a public relations department or relying on the services of outside consultants will obviously depend on the size of the organisation and the nature of the public relations activities it is proposed to undertake.

The carrying out of the advisory part of public relations would seem to be particularly appropriate to consultancy, but the exercise of the executive and continuing aspects of a campaign might be better covered by an internal staff department. An experienced public relations consultant is well qualified to advise an organisation on the pros and cons of the adoption of a campaign or public relations programme, or to investigate and report on the effectiveness of existing activities in this field. Once the recommendations have been adopted, however, the most effective way of implementing the public relations programme is likely to be by the establishment of a public relations department or by the expansion of an existing department.

This does not apply in the case of small or medium-sized companies or organisations, where it is likely to be uneconomic to make staff appointments and to run a separate department. A small organisation will find it more satisfactory to use the services of consultants.

The above views are supported by the action of some leading consultants who often recommend to large organisations which consult them that they should establish internal public relations departments, retaining their services in an advisory capacity. In some instances the consultant seconds staff to form a department within the organisation. They remain employees of the consultant and not of the organisation for which they are working full-time. This may be satisfactory as a short-term measure, but it is open to the criticism that the staff are likely to have divided loyalties and cannot identify themselves completely with the interests of the organisation they serve. On the other hand, a public relations practitioner may sometimes have to give advice or take urgent action which is not particularly acceptable to the management, though it is in their best interests. At such times, it is helpful if the practitioner's judgment is unfettered by anxiety about his personal future in the organisation.

Even organisations with well-established and efficient public relations departments may find occasions when the services of consultants can be employed with advantage. This is likely to occur most frequently when onerous but short-term assignments have to be dealt with. It would be foolish to expand the size of the department to cope with transient difficulties, and it is much more sensible to use the assistance of consultants while the extreme pressure of work lasts. Another example might be when a specialist operation is to be undertaken which is outside the normal work of the department. One instance of this could be parliamentary activity, or, to take another extreme, the arranging of a press fashion show, which requires special skills.

A Parallel with the Legal Profession
Exact parallels from one field to another are difficult to find and may often be misleading, but a somewhat similar state of affairs exists in the manner in which organisations seek legal advice. A small company usually retains a firm of solicitors who will be called in to handle any legal matters requiring attention. A larger concern, however, will often have a solicitor or legal adviser as a member of staff to deal with legal problems which are likely to arise much more frequently. In such cases, an outside adviser, ie a counsel, will be called in for advice when necessary. There is an interesting similarity here to the way in which public relations practice is developing.

Organisation of a Consultancy Practice
The largest public relations consultancy in the United Kingdom is the Central Office of Information. It works only for governmental agencies, and gives public relations advice and carries out executive work in any of the fields and media of public relations. Its staff totals over a thousand and it is thus able to be subdivided into specialist divisions. The smallest public relations consultancy consists of one man, or woman, plus one secretary/shorthand-typist; and

there are many small outfits of this kind. Between these two extremes is to be found an immense variety of types of companies and partnerships.

A factor common to all public relations consultants is that they are called in from outside the employing organisation and have to justify their engagement by the work they carry out. This is both a strength and a weakness. It means that there must be a continuing effort to promote the interests of the client, but it also means that there is a constant need to make reports on work done, and a danger of favouring short-term spectacular projects against less dramatic long-term work that might be more beneficial to the client's interests. Not only does a consultant have to devote a considerable amount of staff time to making reports to existing clients, but there is also the need to contact and make proposals to potential clients.

An organisation approaches one or more consultancies chosen because of introduction from a third party, from advertisements or through hearing about good work that the agency has carried out for another client.

A considerable amount of work is usually necessary in order to prepare a presentation, including a memorandum on the public relations needs of an organisation. It is first necessary to consider whether the particular problems are susceptible to treatment by public relations methods within the time available. It may require a considerable amount of research into the organisation's methods and operation before a considered opinion can be formed. Frank discussion with the client is necessary, and there must be a clear understanding of the desired objectives. It is unreasonable for a client to expect this preliminary work to be carried out by the consultancy firm free of charge; this is forbidden under the IPRA code, and the PRCA recommends against this practice.

The Budget

A consultancy cannot provide a satisfactory service unless the client is prepared to pay an adequate fee. When a very low fee is quoted, it is foolish to expect very much in return. Most consultants consider that it is not possible to provide a comprehensive public relations service for less than £20,000 per year, plus disbursements on photographs, entertainment, travelling, etc. Others fix their minimum fee much higher than this. It is of course possible to provide a limited service for less than £20,000 per year, but in those circumstances the client should know what service he is entitled to receive, otherwise the client may be disappointed and the consultant's reputation suffer. These figures do not apply to limited assignments or where a consultant is retained on an advisory basis. Such contracts would be budgeted and agreed in the light of the circumstances.

A number of public relations consultants have costed their expenditure over several years, and the results suggest that the overheads of a practice are about two and a half times the salaries of the executive staff. Most UK consultants are now basing their fees on this assumption. (This is in line with current practice in the United States, Australia and most other countries.) On this basis, it implies that if a senior executive earning £24,000 per year devoted himself full-time to a client, the fee paid by that client should be at least £84,000 per year. In practice, it is unusual for an executive to devote himself to only one client, and it is necessary to keep accurate records of the time spent by members of the staff on behalf of each client. The fees charged can then be related accurately to the work carried out and can be justified actuarially.

Organisation of a Staff Public Relations Department
It would be foolish to attempt to describe a 'typical' internal public relations department, but there are many factors common to all regardless of the wide disparity in size and in the nature of the activities carried out. (Most of the following points apply equally to the internal arrangements within a public relations consultancy).

The first essential is good organisation so that the best use is made of available staff and facilities. Full use should be made of modern equipment such as recording and copying machines, fax and telex. The major cost in a public relations department is the staff and it is, therefore, desirable to do everything within reason to help the staff work efficiently.

Flexibility is another important point. It is quite impracticable in a small office to split up the work into watertight compartments, and there should be as much doubling up as possible to ensure that important projects continue uninterrupted by illness or vacations.

The qualities which characterise success in public relations are discussed in Chapter 17; but reliability and flexibility are essential, and inefficient staff should not be tolerated since their failings can negate the work of the department. The *tempo* of work is usually fast and there is not time to check whether instructions have been carried out, so absolute reliability is very important. Moreover, unlike many other occupations, in public relations it is seldom possible to do one thing at a time so a flexible, 'unflappable' temperament is necessary.

The head of the department will inevitably impress his personality and his attitude to the work on those who collaborate with him, and since public relations is a very personal business it is unlikely that any two departments will be run in exactly the same way even in similar types of organisation. The only criterion that can be applied in any case is whether the department works efficiently or not.

Many practitioners have had the challenging task of establishing a public relations department in an organisation where nothing of the kind had existed previously. This provides an excellent opportunity of starting in the right way, but the first task is often to educate others in the organisation in order to make them understand the function of public relations and the manner in which it fits in with other departments such as personnel and welfare, labour relations and advertising.

One danger is the tendency to send to the public relations department all queries and matters which do not fit easily into the programme of other departments, or which appear to present little prospect of tangible results. The head of the department must be prepared to resist this attempt to make his department the repository of lost causes, and must be prepared if necessary to take his complaint to the executive head of the organisation.

The point has been made above that the staff should be able to do many jobs, but nevertheless in a large department it is desirable to subdivide into several sections. Flexibility can be maintained by trying to see that staff do not stick in one section for too long at a time, but take a turn in each for periods of perhaps six months.

One subdivision will naturally be the press office. Other sections may deal with publications, including house journals, annual reports; publicity, including films, videos, exhibitions and displays; and a general section which will interest itself in such matters as the corporate image of the firm, community relations, visits, intelligence, etc. Where the size of the operation warrants it, each subdivision should have its own head, each answerable to the head of the department who should take the closest interest in the work of each division without interfering unnecessarily with its day-to-day activities. It is a good plan to give colleagues a sense of responsibility by letting them sign their own correspondence and act on their own initiative as far as possible.

When an organisation is housed under one roof, or at least in the same town, the public relations department is usually sited at headquarters. This is not an ideal arrangement, however, if the headquarters is not in the capital, especially for media relations. This is a problem to which there is no completely satisfactory answer. There is the further difficulty in deciding the best manner in which to organise public relations for a group of companies, or a single company with many works and branches. Probably the best solution is to have a headquarters for the public relations office and press office in the communications centre, eg London or New York, with branch public relations offices in each major works or large branch. However this problem is tackled, it will inevitably mean a great deal of travelling by the senior staff, with the attendant waste of time, but there is no way of avoiding it in these circumstances. Telephone link-ups can be used at times to provide an opportunity for joint discussion.

There is no necessity to fix an annual budget as there is when entering into a contract with outside consultants, but most large organisations cost every aspect of their operations and make an annual allotment to each department. Such a budget takes into account the staff salaries, rent and other overheads and common services, in addition to actual disbursements. This gives a realistic picture of the cost of the public relations department. Sometimes a favourable comparison is made with the cost of using outside consultants by taking into account only actual disbursements and ignoring overheads. When a true comparison is made, the financial difference may be small. When there is only a small budget available for the public relations programme, it is probably possible to secure more experienced services from a consultancy than by engaging full-time staff.

CRISIS PUBLIC RELATIONS
There are occasions when catastrophe—minor or major—demands

immediate and effective action rather like a fire engine or a lifeboat responding to an SOS. This type of public relations practice is usually termed as 'Crisis Public Relations' or 'Crisis Management'.

These crises may be caused by accidents, eg Chernobyl, Bhopal and Piper Alpha. Other problems come from unwanted takeover bids or financial crises.

There are two distinct kinds of public relations crises that can happen, 'known unknowns' and 'unknown unknowns'.

1 Known Unknowns

'Known unknowns' describes the type of misfortune that might occur because of the nature of your business or service. If you manufacture motor cars or capital equipment of any kind 'product recall' is always a possibility. If you are in the chemical or nuclear field a radioactive or lethal discharge is a potential danger. Shipping, railroads and aviation have their known dangers. In all these instances, and many similar fields, it is *known* that a catastrophe may occur but it is *unknown* if or when it will take place.

2 Unknown Unknowns

These are sudden calamitous events that cannot be foreseen by anybody. An example was the 'Tylenol' incident in 1982 in the USA when someone injected cyanide poison into some of these popular headache pill capsules causing a number of deaths. Recently jars of baby food have had to be withdrawn because of criminal adulteration. Other examples can be found in the pharmaceutical industry, where drugs have unexpected dangerous side-effects.

Most of our work as public relations practitioners is predictable and can be planned ahead in an orderly manner. Crisis public relations is a rare requirement and may never affect most of us, but if we are in a field where disasters may occur it is essential to have a plan to meet sudden emergencies.

The priority that should be allocated to a 'crisis plan' will depend on your vulnerability but all companies should pay attention to this question as a form of insurance.

A Typical Crisis Public Relations Plan

The first requirement is a *written* assessment of likely disasters and an appraisal of the company's ability to cope with a major incident.

Based on this report, which must be submitted to and approved by management, it is then possible to take the necessary steps to 'be prepared'.

Effective crisis management depends on three key elements:

1 Agreed company policy for handling emergencies.

2 Tested methods of communication, facilities and equipment.

3 Key personnel trained to take immediate action should a serious incident occur, with designated spokespersons to speak on the company's behalf at press conferences, on the telephone or on television.

1 Company policy

Unless top management fully appreciate the importance of a crisis plan it is very difficult, if not impossible, to prepare a comprehensive public relations programme and to have personnel trained to operate it.

2 Methods of Communication

This starts with the training of key personnel within your own company. This training should include sessions on speaking on the telephone and radio and experience of being interviewed on television.

Trained personnel will require effective means of communication: telephone lines, telex etc. Ordinary facilities are likely to be quite inadequate in an emergency.

3 Key Personnel

Practice sessions are essential if a real state of preparedness is to be achieved. These sessions should be appropriate to the company's possible emergencies. Each practice session should be reviewed and discussed by all concerned and a rerun on video can be very helpful in making the review really informative. If possible, local police, fire brigades and local authorities should be involved in practice sessions.

Disasters may hit at any time of day or night so the designated key personnel must be on 24 hours alert. This means that there must be alternative teams available on a rota.

Should an Emergency Occur

The essential points are: immediate response; giving the media full accurate information; having technical information readily to hand; and doing everything possible for the welfare of victims and their relatives.

Michael Regester, in his excellent book *Crisis Management*, emphasises the importance of 'Tell your own tale', 'Tell it all' and 'Tell it fast'. He quotes Dow Canada's corporate crisis policy:

1 Honesty first, foremost and always.
2 Empathy and compassion.
3 Openness, accessibility and candour.
4 Timeliness.
5 Proactive, not simply reactive.

LEGAL ASPECTS OF PUBLIC RELATIONS PRACTICE

Every practitioner needs a working knowledge of the law that may affect certain aspects of professional work. The following notes* apply to current law in England and Wales, Scottish law differs in some respects.

Defamation

Defamation has been defined as the publication of a statement which tends to lower a person in the estimation of right-thinking members of society generally, or which tends to make them shun or avoid that person. It is a civil wrong which can be the subject of an action for damages, with or without an injunction to prohibit further publication.

Sometimes material issued by a public relations practitioner, however innocently, can arouse complaints of defamation.

In England (but not in Scotland) there are two kinds of defamation—libel and slander. A defamatory statement is libel if it is in a permanent form (such as writing or even radio and television) and slander if it is only transitory (such as spoken words).

---

*These notes are extracted, by permission, from The Institute of Public Relations Guideline No 1.

A statement is actionable as a libel or slander if:

(a) it is defamatory

(b) it is false (but the law presumes this unless the contrary is proved)

(c) it is understood to refer to the plaintiff, ie the person who claims to have been defamed

(d) it has been published, ie made known to at least one other person other than the plaintiff.

It is important to remember that a statement which is, on the face of it, quite harmless, may be defamatory when made to people who have 'background' knowledge. For example, to say that a person was useless at public relations would probably be defamatory only if it were made to someone who happened to know that the person referred to was a professional public relations man! This is what lawyers call an 'innuendo', a hidden sting to the statement. Every publication of the defamation is a fresh cause of action. If you write a press release containing a libel, and send it to a news agency, that is a publication, for which you could be sued. If the news agency issues the story to a newspaper, the agency could be sued. And if the newspaper prints the statement, the editor, printer and publisher could all be sued.

In a libel action the plaintiff can win without proving that he has actually suffered damage; the law presumes that he has. In slander, a plaintiff must prove actual damage, except in four cases: a) imputation of a serious criminal offence; b) imputation of a contagious or infectious disease, which would cause the person concerned to be shunned by others; c) imputation of unchastity or adultery to a woman or girl; d) perhaps the most important in practice—imputation of unfitness, dishonesty or incompetence in the plaintiff's carrying out of his office, profession or business.

Possible defences to an action for defamation
These include:

(a) Assent. If the plaintiff has agreed, directly or by implication to publication of a statement about himself which is true on the face of it, the defendant is not liable. Moral: get written approval from the subject (as well as from your client or employer) for any questionable statement.

(b) Unintentional defamation. In the case of words published innocently, the defendant is not liable to pay damages if he offers to publish a reasonable correction and apology and pays the plaintiff's costs. This applies in two cases: i) if the publisher of the statement did not intend it to refer to the plaintiff (eg he meant to refer to someone with a similar name) or ii) if the statement was not defamatory on the face of it, and the publisher did not know it could have a defamatory meaning. In either case, reasonable care must have been taken.

(c) Justification—that is, truth. If a defendant can prove that the statement (including any innuendo) was true, he is not liable—for the law will not protect a reputation which is not deserved. To say that the statement is a correct report of what someone else wrote or said is not enough (except in special circumstances which are privileged).

(d) Fair comment. A statement which is fair comment on a matter of public interest, is not defamatory, provided it is an expression of opinion which is based on fact.

(e) Privilege. This is a big subject. There are two types of privilege, absolute and qualified. Absolute privilege means that no liability for defamation ever exists in the circumstances to which it applies. Anything said in Parliament, or any relevant statement in a UK law court, is in this category.

Qualified privilege exempts from liability only if the statement is made honestly both as to what is said and the means by which it is said. This applies to fair and accurate report of Parliamentary or most UK legal proceedings, and of various other matters; another example is a statement made by an employer in giving a reference about a former employee. Qualified privilege may cease to be a defence if it can be shown that the report or statement was activated by malice. These examples are by no means exhaustive, but merely indicate general principles.

Other damaging statements

Defamation covers statements which damage a company or person's reputation. False statements of other kinds can, of course, damage a person's business or other interests. They are actionable if made with dishonest or other improper motive; but damage must be proved, unless the statement is in writing or other permanent form and calculated to cause financial loss or calculated to cause financial damage in respect of the person's office, profession, etc.

Copyright

Copyright is the exclusive right to copy or use in certain other ways any 'literary, dramatic, musical or artistic work'. Most of the law governing copyright in the United Kingdom is contained in the Copyright Act, 1956.

A public relations practitioner may well have to utilise reproduced material of one kind or another. So it is advisable to bear the following notes in mind.

The phrase 'literary, dramatic, musical or artistic work' is interpreted very widely. It includes practically every form of written or printed material (even, for instance, directories or timetables); photographs; gramophone records; tape recordings; and sound and television broadcasts. Although there are some exceptions, it is safest to assume that any written or pictorial material is subject to copyright unless you know otherwise.

Copyright exists in the *form* of the work, including the arrangement and expression of the facts or ideas in it. There is no copyright in facts or ideas in themselves. So there is no copyright in news—but there is copyright in the text of a news story or a press release, and for that matter in typographical design.

Ownership of the copyright in Britain is automatic provided certain circumstances exist. No special steps have to be taken to register work. To gain copyright protection in countries overseas certain steps are frequently required such as the inclusion in a book of the name of the copyright owner with the symbol 'C' in a circle.

The owner of the copyright is normally the person who wrote, compiled or otherwise created the work (note, for instance, that the copyright in a letter is held by the writer and not the addressee). There are exceptions to this, and three of them are specially important in public relations. They are: (1) Photographs: if a photograph is commissioned the copyright is owned by the person or firm who commissioned it; in the case of cine films, this is not the case, unless the maker of the film assigns the copyright to the person or organisation who commissioned it. (2) Broadcasts: copyright in the broadcast itself always belongs to the BBC or IBA unless there is an agreement to the contrary; copyright in, for instance, the text is normally held by the BBC or the programme company concerned. (3) If you write, take photographs or produce other copyright work as part of your employment, the copyright normally belongs to your employer, not to you (in the case of people employed by newspapers or magazines only the newspaper or magazine rights go to the employer, however). Employment here means full-time work.

When in doubt seek advice: ownership of copyright is too big a subject to cover fully here. Moreover, in every case it is open to the owner of copyright to assign it or license someone else to exercise all or part of his right.

Contracts

Contracts affect almost every business activity. Consultancy agreements, contracts of employment, the commissioning of photographs or artwork, the ordering of print: all these are everyday examples in public relations.

A contract is an agreement which can be enforced by law, or for the breach of which the law will provide a remedy. Contracts in formal language, signed, witnessed and sealed are only a small proportion of legally enforceable agreements. A contract need not even be in writing—it can be in spoken words, or implied by actions, such as purchasing goods in a shop. Frequently an exchange of letters, such as between a consultant and his client, is evidence of a binding contract.

Agreement between the parties, express or implied. To reach an agreement there must be an offer on one side, and an unconditional acceptance, expressed or implied on the other. An offer can be revoked at any time before it has been accepted.

Intent to create legal relations. A preliminary discussion between a consultant and a potential client, or a public relations man and a freelance or printer whom he is thinking of employing, are usually not intended by either side to be binding—any more than an invitation to dinner would be. It is important to determine clearly the point at which a specific offer is made, with the intention that acceptance will form a legally enforceable agreement.

Consideration—the legal term for 'value given' or *'quid pro quo'*—is necessary in most forms of contract. A promise or undertaking can be valid consideration: and as long as what is given is of *some* value, the law is not concerned with whether it is 'fair' or not—that is for the parties to agree.

Terms of the contract will often be implied by law if they are not expressly agreed by the parties. If terms are agreed, however, they must be precise—if they are vague, they cannot be enforced at law. It is sensible to reach clear agreement on such matters as notice periods, fees, and the extent of work to be done or goods or services provided.

Breach of confidence
Although there is no copyright in facts or ideas as such, misuse of confidential information can be the subject of an action for breach of confidence. The court can award damages or grant an injunction to stop further misuse.

Summary
Consideration of these legal aspects of practice should be compared with the provisions of Codes of Professional Conduct. (See Appendix I).

METHODS OF PUBLIC RELATIONS PRACTICE
The methods of carrying out a public relations programme will be very similar regardless of whether an organisation uses the services of outside consultants, has its own internal department, or employs a combination of these two arrangements.

The media of public relations are the tools which are available to carry out the public relations programme and the various media are described in detail in Part II of this book. These chapters set out the fundamental issues involved in the use of each medium, but many years of practice are necessary before achieving mastery of all these methods of communication.

The way in which public relations is practised depends very much on the field of interest of the organisation, although the basic principles are similar. In Part III, practice in a number of different fields is discussed in detail.

Public relations practice is now generally understood and used in most countries of the world. The theory and philosophy is the same world wide but the practice of public relations depends on local conditions—economic, cultural and religious.

Part 2

Methods of Public Relations

3 *Media Relations*

THE ETHOS OF PRESS RELATIONS

In 1906 an early example of crisis public relations was when Ivy Leadbetter Lee was appointed to help the Anthracite Coal Roads and Mine Company cope with an imminent strike.

Young Ivy Lee issued his historic 'Declaration of Principles' to city editors of newspapers along with his first statement to the press. He wrote:

This is not a secret press bureau. All our work is done in the open. We aim to supply news. This is not an advertising agency; if you think any of our matter ought properly to go to your business office, do not use it. Our matter is accurate. Further details on any subject treated will be supplied promptly, and any editor will be assisted most cheerfully in verifying directly any statement of fact. Upon inquiry, full information will be given to any editor concerning those on whose behalf an article is sent out. In brief, our plan is, frankly and openly, on behalf of the business concerns and public institutions, to supply to the press and public of the United States prompt and accurate information concerning subjects which it is of value and interest to the public to know about. Corporations and public institutions give out much information in which the news point is lost to view. Nevertheless, it is quite as important to the public to have this news as it is to the establishments themselves to give it currency. I send out only matter every detail of which I am willing to assist any editor in verifying for himself. I am always at your service for the purpose of enabling you to obtain more complete information concerning any of the subjects brought forward in my copy.

This statement ushered in a revolution in relations between business and the public. 'The public be damned' attitude was increasingly replaced by 'the public be informed'.

Media or press relations is probably the most important single part of public relations but it is only a part, and it is important that this distinction should be understood. It is unfortunate that both public relations and press relations are often referred to as PR in the UK as this leads to confusion. The problem is not common in the USA, however, since the term media relations is more often used.

Two-way Communication

Media relations is essentially a two-way operation. It is the link between an organisation and the press, radio and television. On the one hand, the organisation supplies information and provides facilities to the media on request, and on the other it takes steps to initiate comment and news. Confidence and respect between an organisation and the media are the necessary basis for good relations.

Even in this radio and television age, public opinion is still moulded mainly by what is read in the national, provincial and trade press. It is essential to respect the integrity and traditional freedom of the press—a freedom which gives it so much of its significance—but it is possible to seek the cooperation of the press for the furtherance of public relations objectives.

Basis of Media Relations

The best policy is to take the media into your confidence at all times. Tell the press as much as possible, even confidential matters, and then tell them which items must not be published and why.

It is wise to cultivate a balanced outlook towards press comment. The popular press will always prefer something sensational to news of steady progress, however important the latter may be to the national regional or local prosperity. There are, however, many opportunities for securing useful mention in the press if the needs of newspapers and periodicals are understood.

All papers are ready to publish hard news even if their treatment of it may vary considerably according to editorial policy and the type of readership. A newsworthy story or item will always be welcomed by the press, and it is only necessary to ensure that the press shall receive the item expeditiously and accurately.

Today, however, a major part of press space is devoted to articles and features that give the background to the news, or to articles and features about matters of current or general interest. It is here that there exists such an excellent opportunity of seeking the cooperation of journalists to advance particular interests. They require a continual supply of ideas and subjects on which to base their journalistic flow, and they are usually only too ready to listen to constructive suggestions. This situation might appear to open a door to undue influence, or even bribery, but it is rare for there to be any suggestion of corruption, indeed, undue hospitality often results in defeating its purpose.

A new professional respect is slowly developing between representatives of the press and public relations practitioners. The press is beginning to recognise the value of having contacts within organisations which can provide information quickly and accurately. Competent public relations practitioners, in turn, respect the media representatives' role in providing balanced information to the public and understand the problems of expediency and limited space. Another factor may be the recognition by the press of the role of public relations practitioners in educating management to the importance of honesty and full disclosure.

THE PRESS OFFICER

It is often stated that press officers hinder the press in securing news and stories, and that hand-outs have had a bad effect on standards of reporting. A press officer's duty is to assist the press, and if he acts as a barrier he is failing in his job. For every press officer who hinders, there are hundreds who render invaluable service to the press by day *and* night. Hand-outs are a useful method of giving information to the press, but journalists should not use them *verbatim*—if they do so the responsibility is theirs, and theirs alone.

A press office is not a policy-making body; it exists to serve the press. The size and establishment should be related to the calls likely to be made on its services, but it should be large enough to cope easily with normal requirements and to be able to overcome the occasional panic. It is essential for there to be arrangements for answering night inquiries for the benefit of the national dailies. Mention has already been made of the two prime considerations in press relations: speed and accuracy. If a reporter telephones with a query he needs the answer quickly. If he cannot be given the answer, he should be told so and if possible referred to another source for the information he is seeking. If an editor asks for photographs he should be told whether they are available or when they can be supplied. Whatever arrangement is made for supplying information or photographs, it should be kept *to the minute*. It is exasperating for the press to have to ring up repeatedly to ask for the promised information.

The need for accuracy is obvious, but a positive approach is desirable to look out for possible sources of error and to avoid them. Names or statistics given on the telephone may easily be misheard, and care should be taken to ensure accuracy. Some reporters will get the figures wrong regardless of the care exercised but every effort should be taken to avoid contributing to the possibility.

Two very important factors in press relations are timing and distribution: choosing the psychological moment to release news, and seeing that it reaches the right people.

Press relations is an exacting job if it is done with due care and conscientiousness. In a large organisation, it is undesirable for the press officer to undertake other major responsibilities in his organisation, as they are bound to interfere with the efficient performance of his job as press officer.

The present custom of recruiting press officers from the ranks of journalists does not meet with universal approval. At least one leading National newspaper editor has publicly expressed his dislike of seeing ex-colleagues installed as press officers. His view was that press officers should *issue* news and that journalists should *write* the stories. He mistrusted the tendency to hand out stories already written in a form suitable for publication, as he felt it interfered with the duty of journalists to seek out the full facts and to write their own interpretation of them.

The main justification for having a press officer is to ensure that the press can receive prompt attention to their needs. It is a negation of this if the press officer is so busy that he is seldom available to speak on the telephone. In too many cases it is more difficult to reach the press officer on the telephone than it is to speak to the managing director! This situation is more likely to arise when the head of the public relations department acts also as press officer.

Some press officers carry on happily in the belief that they are providing an excellent service to the press. This may be so, but often it is not. A good idea is to ask members of the press whether they are satisfied with the service they are receiving or whether there are suggestions they would care to make. The results of such inquiries may be very revealing.

To establish satisfactory cooperation with journalists it is necessary to understand how they work and how they think. It is not essential for a press officer to have been a journalist himself, but if he has not had personal experience he should take the trouble to visit one or more newspaper offices and to study the conditions under which the press operates. It is essential to read regularly as many different papers as possible, and it is also useful to try to write articles and features for the experience this will provide.

It is desirable to maintain regular contact with journalists by sending them background information, and not merely to approach them when some 'story' has broken. It cannot be emphasised too strongly that the establishment of friendly relations with the media on a continuing basis will yield good dividends.

It is also essential that an officer has a complete understanding of the goals and mission of the corporation or organisation he represents so that a planned programme of news releases and feature articles can be carried out which will reinforce the total public relations programme of an institution.

If the nature of the organisation is such that it may possibly be involved in disasters or emergencies, it is essential to organise routine procedures to deal with such situations. The press should know the name of the person who will act as spokesman under such conditions and where to contact him. Journalists should be given factual information in emergencies as fully and as quickly as possible, as they are the direct link with the public. See page 30 for a discussion of crisis public relations.

Providing an Information Service
In return for publishing news sent by the public relations department of an organisation, the media will expect to be able to seek information from the organisation about itself or its industry. In some instances this may be for background information, but in others it may lead to press publicity beneficial to the organisation's interests. At times, unfortunately, the press may be digging into

matters which would be best left uncovered. In all these cases, it is desirable to help the inquirers as much as possible. If the subject is a delicate one, journalists may agree not to pursue the issue if they are told the reasons frankly. Concealment, on the other hand, is likely to inflame their news sense and to make them keener than ever to pursue the scent.

In giving information to a journalist it is important to make it clear whether the information can be quoted as an official statement, and attributed to a particular individual or to 'a spokesman' of the organisation. The journalist may be told, on the other hand, that he can use the information provided no source is quoted; or that the information is strictly confidential and nothing may appear in print.

Only on very few occasions do journalists abuse confidences, and when this does occur it is often because the need for secrecy was not explained. There is, moreover, a complication if the newspaper receives the information from another source after it has been given it in confidence by the organisation mainly concerned. This presents a very difficult decision for the news editor, especially as sometimes an organisation tells journalists certain facts in confidence with the express intention of muzzling the press should the news leak out. Where mutual confidence exists between the press officer and the press, these difficulties seldom arise, and when they do it is possible to find a satisfactory solution or to agree on a compromise.

The organised 'leak' has become quite a popular device, especially with governments. When the press publishes 'leaked' information, it arouses public reaction—favourable or unfavourable. If the adverse reaction is strong, the government then denies the report. Such practices should not be recommended or condoned by public relations professionals as they undermine the confidence of the public, raise serious ethical questions, and result in a loss of respect from the press. If the press officer is involved, a loss of credibility will result. The practice also exposes the organisation to charges of favouritism in the release of information.

All newspapers and periodicals, however frequently they are published, aim to publish stories and features that are not to be found in the pages of their competitors. The difficulty in securing 'scoops' is one of the aspects of modern journalism which is often blamed on public relations. The reason lies rather in the increased complexity of life and to a certain extent on shorter working hours.

These factors make it more difficult for journalists to meet the men and women who make news.

A problem arises when an organisation is preparing facts or figures to issue coinciding with an event to take place in the near future, and a journalist—by chance or deduction—hits on the story and rings up for confirmation. There are only two possible ways of answering the inquiry: the truth or a lie. It may be tempting to deny the whole story, but to take this line will destroy the possibility of future cooperation with this newspaper or journal. It is essential, both on moral grounds and in the interests of expediency, to give the information requested and to explain why the story was to have been issued on a particular occasion. A further problem now arises: as the story has been uncovered, should it be released generally to the press or should the journalist who hit on it be allowed to reap the benefits of his initiative and perspicacity? Except where questions of privilege may arise, it is wise to let that journalist have at least a good start before releasing the information. If it is not a matter affecting policy, it is desirable to let the journalist have his 'scoop' unchallenged.

A somewhat similar question arises when a decision is made as to which journals news should be issued on any particular subject. Selective issuing of information to the media arouses indignation on the part of those journals not selected, and as a rule it is far wiser to make a general release to all newspapers and periodicals likely to be interested.

The practice of some executives in taking a positive delight in barking 'No Comment' in response to press inquiries should be strongly deprecated. It is rude and unproductive. It is much better to try to pursue a dialogue about topics that *can* be discussed.

When telephoning a journalist or an editor make the call yourself. They are busy people and may not appreciate having to hang on while your secretary locates you.

Organisation of an Information Office

The size of a press office staff may be anything from one or two to twenty or more men and women; obviously, then, it is not possible to discuss here every kind of press office, since the form will depend on the type of organisation to be served. There are some general observations which can be made usefully, leaving the reader to adapt the general principles to meet individual circumstances. In general, the following points apply equally to press relations carried out by a consultancy.

In large organisations the press office will often be a subsection of the public relations department, with the press officer under the jurisdiction of the head of the department. In smaller set-ups, the chief public relations executive and the press officer will probably be the same person. The press officer will usually act as the spokesman for the organisation, but obviously he should take guidance on policy from the head of the public relations department who in turn is answerable to management.

It is desirable that all press inquiries should be channelled through the press office, and that there should always be someone there competent to deal with anything that is likely to arise. It is relevant to note that this single-channel method of dealing with press inquiries came into being at the request of the newspapermen themselves and was not a public relations invention.

Although the press officer should act as spokesman for his organisation on ordinary matters, it is much better for the chief executive to speak for his organisation on matters of vital concern to the nation or to his organisation. It is creditable that so many top businessmen increasingly find the time to appear on radio and television and to take part in public affairs. This is public relations of the best kind, and it should be the constant effort of press officers to get their senior executives to accept their responsibilities in this respect.

The work of a press officer falls into three categories:

1   Issuing news and initiating articles, features and reports.

2   Answering press inquiries and providing a comprehensive information service.

3   Monitoring the press, radio and television, and evaluating the results; taking steps where appropriate to correct mis-statements or to initiate counter publicity.

Issuing news and information

It is the duty of the public relations staff to do everything possible to facilitate the flow of news from the organisation. This may involve a considerable degree of educational work, for top management may take a great deal of convincing that it is desirable to keep the media fully informed.

Press offices usually work under pressure of day-to-day requirements, but it is essential to plan ahead since some operations will be likely to require detailed planning. The timing of important events is usually known in advance, and special steps should be taken well ahead. If necessary, help should be sought from outside sources to ensure that a special event will be dealt with adequately when the time comes. Some firms specialise in providing such short-term services.

The placing of articles is a very useful means of bringing the organisation and its activities to the notice of a wide public. All editors are interested to receive suggestions for articles, and if the idea appeals it will result in either a request for an article to be submitted or for facilities to be provided for a journalist to obtain information on which to base an article. This practice is growing in industry, where it is often considered most useful for the technical staff of the organisation to contribute papers to the appropriate technical journals. Some companies attach so much importance to this point that they have appointed technical journalists to their staff whose sole job is to encourage the writing of papers by senior staff and to arrange publication in suitable journals.

In many companies, it is the rule that all requests for articles from members of the company should be dealt with by the press office. This is a perfectly reasonable internal arrangement, but if interpreted too rigidly can lead to friction with the press. If an editor writes to the chairman of a company he will not take offence if he receives a polite letter from the press officer stating that the chairman has asked him to deal with the matter. In some instances, however, the editor receives a peremptory letter from the press officer demanding that all future letters of this kind should be sent to the press officer and that on no account should the chief executive or members of the board be approached direct.

Issuing Press Releases

The most usual way of issuing information to the press is by the writing of a *news or press release*. This is then sent by post, by hand or electronically to the various newspapers and periodicals, and to radio and television news offices. It should also be communicated to the news agencies, who have direct contact with the main newspaper offices in the country. If the story has overseas interest, it should be sent to the Central Office of Information and to the overseas news agencies which have offices in London, and to the BBC external services. *(See* Chapter 8 for further discussion of this aspect.)

The news agencies will edit the release and will not send it out in its entirety, so it is always worth while sending out the full release as widely as possible even though some of the recipients will have had it over the wire earlier.

It is essential to keep an uptodate *distribution list* so that releases can be sent out without delay. Most organisations will need several lists—each appropriate to different types of release. Keeping the lists uptodate is a boring task and is often left to a junior. This is a mistake, as it is essential to have an accurate list at all times. One method is to keep sets of envelopes ready addressed so that it is merely a question of selecting the right set of envelopes and inserting the release. It is usual to address the release to the news editor in the case of national newspapers, but when it is for other papers it can be sent to the editor. In some cases it may be desirable to send it to the city editor, women's editor, social editor, picture editor, etc.

Where a press office is responsible for a group of companies with varied interests, the compilation of press lists may become very complex and it may be necessary to have a large number of different lists for use as appropriate. One solution to this problem is to use a computer retrieval system.

There are a number of specialist companies which are geared to produce and distribute releases either by post, by courier or electronically.

A large press office will probably prefer to send out its own releases, and the lists can be kept up to date with the help of *Willing's Press Guide* or *Benn's Media Directory,* published in two parts, United Kingdom and International. Since these are published annually, it is advisable to watch the trade press weekly for changes of address, new publications, etc.

Hollis Press and Public Relations Annual is also a most valuable book of reference. It is published annually and is a most comprehensive guide to UK information sources and public relations consultancies world wide.

Writing a News or Press Release

In preparing a release it is well to remember that it will have to compete for attention with a great quantity of similar communications which editors receive daily. For this reason it is a good plan to have a printed heading which will identify the source of the press release. Such headings are often in colour, and should be in the organisation's house style if it has one. Otherwise, a distinctive well designed heading is likely to be most effective.

It must be remembered, however, that if news releases are poorly written and contain little news value on a regular basis, the distinctive heading and organisation identification will also earmark the release for the editor's spike or waste bin.

The name and address of the sender should be clearly indicated, together with the name, telephone number and extension of the person who can give further information if it is required. The night telephone number should also be given, as national newspapers work through the night.

The date should be given on the release, and it is usual to mark it 'immediate' or to state a release time. The word 'embargo' is necessary if it is a summary of a speech which is to be delivered at a certain time; in general, however, embargoes should not be used except when they are essential, eg when parliamentary privilege is involved, or when a lengthy and complicated report has to be digested. Embargoes are respected by the press when it is in their own interest; when they are applied to comparatively unimportant news stories, some papers will ignore the story altogether as a gentle reproof and others will ignore the embargo! It is thus far wiser to mark the release 'immediate' and to send it out so that it reaches the press at the appropriate time.

The special problems of dealing with parliamentary and governmental news are discussed in Chapter 14.

When press releases are issued by a consultant on behalf of a client, this fact should be clearly indicated and the name and address of the client stated, together with information as to where further details can be sought.

The release should be typed on one side of the sheet in double spacing, of course, and with generous margins.

The release should be headed with a title which explains the subject. It is *not* necessary to think up a clever headline—leave this to the sub-editor. It is usual to make the first paragraph tell the story and then to proceed to give details in the following paragraphs. This is a good plan, but should not be carried to extremes: far more important is to tell the story logically and clearly, omitting unnecessary adjectives and elaboration.

Anyone who can write good plain English can write a good press release, but experience makes one wonder whether the ability to write good English is as rare as the possession of common sense. Above all, avoid the use of superlatives.

There is no mystique about writing a press release; it is merely a communication between two people and should be presented in the way most likely to achieve the desired result. If it is badly done it will undoubtedly find its resting place on the spike or in the wastepaper basket. It will find a similar resting place if there is no useful information or news in it. However much it is disguised, a 'puff' will be recognised by the recipient, and not only will it be torn up but it is likely to prejudice the reaction to future releases from the same source.

The prime requirement of a release is that it should make its meaning absolutely plain and be free from ambiguity. Many releases of a technical nature that are sent out are far from clear and require a telephone call to the sender to elucidate the details. When this happens, the press office often attributes the ambiguity to the technical people who insisted on certain phrases. This may be true, but no press officer should issue a release which he himself cannot understand, however much the technical people insist.

Sometimes a press release must run to several pages to cover the subject, but whenever possible it should be kept to one or two sheets, ie about three to five hundred words in all. Other information relating to the release can be appended on separate sheets, and this is preferable to making the actual release too long.

A release that is suitable for the national press is unlikely to be equally satisfactory for issue to the technical press, and it is often desirable to prepare two or more versions. It is also quite a good idea to prepare supplementary facts that can be given to members of the press ringing up for additional information. By this means the reports appearing in different sections of the press are likely to be more varied in their nature.

If individuals are mentioned, give their full names and state any official positions held. Explain the purpose of any organisation if it is not generally known. Give precise figures in preference to approximations whenever possible.

Sometimes photographs are sent with press releases. Since prints are expensive, it may be advisable to indicate that photographs are available on certain subjects rather than to enclose copies with each release. A good plan is to include miniature copies of available prints.

Some rules for preparing a news release

1 Use only one side of the paper.

2 Have good margins, left and right.

3 Always use double-spacing.

4 Typewritten copy is essential, except in real emergency.

5 Do NOT underline anything, not even the heading. Editors prefer to decide themselves what they wish to emphasise.

6 Paragraphs should be indented except the first opening paragraph which should not be indented.

7 A news release should have a headline which should describe the news story but not attempt to be 'clever'. Editors prefer to write their own headlines.

8 The news release paper can have a printed heading which details the name and address of the organisation sending out the release. It should include the telephone number (day and night if possible). This information should be repeated at the end of the release including the name(s) of persons available to give further information on request.

9 If a public relations consultancy is issuing the news release on behalf of a client, this should be indicated clearly.

10 When possible, news releases should be kept short so that they will go on one single sheet. If this is not possible, put 'more' at the bottom right hand of the page and number all pages.

11 The release should be dated and it is useful to repeat the date at the bottom left hand of the last page of a long release. The date is normally the date when the release will be received. It is not necessary to write 'immediate' as this is obvious.

12 Embargoes should be avoided. It may be necessary if it is a

summary of a speech which is to be delivered at a certain time; in general, however, embargoes should not be used except when they are essential, eg when parliamentary privilege is involved, or when a lengthy and complicated report has to be digested. Embargoes are respected by the press when it is in their own interest; when they are applied to run of the mill news stories, some papers will ignore the story altogether and others will ignore the embargo! Remember that you cannot enforce any embargo except with the ready cooperation of the recipient.

13 Use capitals as little as possible. Never put whole words in capitals. Capitals should be restricted to people's names, place names and other proper nouns like company and product names.

14 Write UN, BBC, WHO, UK and not U.N., B.B.C., W.H.O., U.K. Publications usually leave out full points except at the end of sentences.

15 Dates are usually expressed as January 6, 1983 and not 6th January 1983.

16 Numbers should be spelt out from one to nine and given in figures above nine. Use 'thousand' or 'million' for very large numbers. Use figures for measurements, dates, prices or street numbers. If a sentence has to start with a number it must be spelt out.

17 Per cent should be preferred to %. 30 deg C is a preferred style for temperatures.

18 Restrict quotation marks (' ') to spoken speech. Do not use for brand names.

Press Conferences and Receptions

The holding of a press conference has become an accepted means of issuing information to the press, and it is very effective if used with discretion. Some organisations, however, never miss an excuse for calling a press conference or holding a reception for the press. This may be due to the managing director fancying his ability as an orator, or to the insistence of public relations consultants who wish to show activity on behalf of their clients.

A press conference should never be called merely to hand out a document or information which could be issued equally well by a release. The main justification for holding a conference is to show models or other solid items or when the subject is an important one likely to elicit questions from the journalists present. Press conferences are also an excellent method of imparting background information 'off the record' when it would be inadvisable to set it out in print. Do not—as sometimes happens—forget to tell the press if the information given out is 'off the record'.

The press welcomes invitations to cocktail receptions provided there is news to be obtained or an opportunity provided to talk informally with senior members of an organisation. It is no longer true—if it ever was—that the press will go anywhere for a drink: lavish hospitality is never an adequate substitute for news.

If it is necessary to hold a press conference at very short notice, news editors may be telephoned individually or the news agencies may be asked to announce the time and place in the material sent over the wire to newspapers.

An invitation to a press conference should normally be sent out a week in advance. It should state clearly the reason for holding it, and if possible, the names of the principal speakers. It is desirable to give sufficient details to make the editor feel the event is worth covering, but not to divulge so much of the story that it might be considered unnecessary to attend. Clear information as to the venue, date and time should be given, of course—it is remarkable how often one or other of these essential points is omitted. The venue of the press conference should usually be in London, even if the headquarters of the organisation is elsewhere. If it has to be held outside London—at a new factory, for example—somewhat different conditions apply and the provincial press would be very important. Most of these papers have direct links with the nationals.

If the conference is of general interest, it is impossible to select a time of day that will suit every section of the press. The morning newspapers are not keen on carrying a story which has already appeared the previous evening in the papers and on the radio or television news. The usual times for conferences are 11.00 to 11.30 hrs or 14.30 to 15.00 hrs. If the subject is a technical one it is probably preferable to hold the conference in the morning, as this will give the dailies time to prepare a full report, and a short report in the evening newspapers will not worry them. Morning newspapers go to press so early these days that it is unwise to hold a press conference later than 15.00 hrs unless it is intended mainly for the weekly trade and technical press.

Choosing a suitable day is also very important. In some cases there is no choice possible, as the announcement has to be made on a certain day. Where there is latitude, however, care should be taken to avoid clashing with any other events that may keep the press away and may compete unfairly for prominence in the papers. It would be foolish, for example, for a motor accessory firm to hold a press conference at the same time as press day at the Motor Show. This is an imaginary example, but similar instances do occur showing remarkable lack of forethought. Fridays are always bad days for the national newspapers.

Special arrangements have to be made with monthly journals, since they often go to press several months ahead. This applies particularly to popular monthlies and women's journals.

Some editors reply to invitations to press conferences, others do not, so it is seldom possible to know the likely attendance. It is always better to have too many chairs than not enough. If the conference is called for 11.00 hrs the first arrivals may come up to twenty minutes earlier, and it creates a very bad impression if the room is still being arranged. It is usual to have one or more tables by the entrance at which the press sign in and receive hand-outs and photographs. If a large attendance is expected, there should be several members of staff dealing with the arrivals to avoid queues. A personal welcome from the press officer or his assistants puts the journalists in a good humour from the outset.

There is no need for elaborate arrangements, but it is helpful if there is a raised dais for the platform party. They should have their names indicated on cards in front of them, and the wording should be large enough to be read from the back of the hall. All members of the public relations staff on duty should wear badges with their names; this is an obvious point that is often overlooked.

The public relations executive who is in charge of the conference will usually call the meeting to order and introduce the chairman or chief executive. Alternatively, the chairman may use his gavel to obtain silence and then carry straight on with his address. The success or otherwise of the conference will depend to a great extent on the speaking ability of the chairman and others supporting him. If the chairman is a poor speaker it is difficult to surmount this obstacle completely; the only hope is to try to persuade him to give a short introduction and to ask others to elaborate the various points.

Whenever it is practicable, a briefing meeting should be held beforehand at which it will be agreed what shall be said to the press and how likely questions shall be dealt with. A briefing of this kind is most helpful in promoting the success of the conference, but there is no need to carry it to extremes. (At one press conference, the chairman had at the end of his typed speech answers to a number of questions which various members of the audience had been primed to ask. Unfortunately the chairman read on at the end of the speech and did not stop until he had read out all the answers! It is quite unnecessary to plant questions. If the speeches from the platform are so comprehensive that few questions result, this should be taken as a measure of success, not as a reflection of any kind.)

If the conference is called for 11.00 hrs it should start within five or ten minutes of that time and the speeches should be kept fairly short, particularly if there are likely to be many questions. It is often usual to offer a drink at the end of the proceedings, and is some cases a buffet lunch is provided. The invitation should indicate clearly the nature of hospitality, if any, to be provided.

If photographs are available they should be given out in protected envelopes, unless all the press information is handed out in a special folder. A plastic document case with nylon zip is often used to hold the press kit, and this is appreciated especially when the name of the donating organisation is not printed right across the case in large letters.

Copies of all speeches should be available at the conference, and steps taken subsequently to send copies to papers or journals that were not represented.

Most of the above comments apply also to press receptions, except that the proceedings are much less formal and usually take place in the evening. Since they are *informal* occasions, it is illogical to have a toastmaster to announce the names of guests.

There is a growing tendency to invite many outsiders to press conferences and receptions—outsiders, that is, in the sense that they are not press. This is not to be encouraged, as it tends to interfere with the primary purpose of the function and is often resented by the media representatives.

Facility Visits

It is human to be impressed more by what one sees than by what one hears, and for this reason visits to factories or installations have an important part to play in public relations. Such visits fall into three main categories: visits by buyers or important business contacts, open days for the public, and press tours.

There is no need to discuss the first group, and visits by the public will be dealt with in greater detail in Chapter 15. The question of press visits, however, is both an interesting and a complex one.

It is common practice to issue individual invitations to editors or journalists, or to invite small groups of the press; but when a major event takes place, such as when a new factory is opened or a new power station commissioned, it is often the practice to issue invitations to the national, local, trade and technical press, and to the radio and television companies. The invitation list will naturally depend on the object of the exercise and what it is hoped to achieve. Whatever the section of the press chosen, it is desirable to ensure that invitations are sent to every journal in that category.

Facility visits are both an excellent method of securing the interest and cooperation of the press, and a very effective means of antagonising them if the arrangements are slapdash or if they go away feeling their journey was not really necessary.

A visit to a manufacturer's works or demonstration often involves a whole day away from the office, with possibly an early start and a late return home. It is essential that there should be sufficient advantage to gain from the visit to compensate for this effort. An abundance of liquor and an excellent lunch will not be regarded as an adequate return by the press unless they are able to see something new or worthwhile on the visit.

A facility visit begins when the invitations are sent out, and these should state clearly the nature of the visit and give all essential data. As much detail as possible should be given about times of trains or aeroplanes, meeting points, hotels, expected time of return to starting point, etc. It is also important to state clearly on the invitation or the accompanying letter whether the sponsors of the visit are providing free transport, hotel accommodation or meals.

It is not essential to provide free travel, but it has become usual for this to be done on industrial visits. Government departments and official bodies are rarely able to offer free travel or hospitality. The essential point is to make the position clear on this matter, as it may in some instances influence the editor's decision to send a representative or not. Having to pay the expenses will not prevent a large attendance if the story is likely to be a good one. On one occasion, a trade association took a party of about twenty technical editors to visit a continental exhibition. The association made all the arrangements for air travel, hotel accommodation, etc, and made an inclusive charge. The charge did not prevent a very high acceptance rate of those invited.

The invitation should indicate the latest date for the replies to be sent, and it is helpful if a stamped addressed card or envelope is enclosed. When acceptances have been received, it is desirable that they should be acknowledged and information given as to when further details will be sent to those taking part in the visit.

In certain circumstances there may be a choice of travel. If time permits, it is a good idea to ask those invited to state their preference so that arrangements may be made in accordance with the majority wish.

If an aeroplane is chartered to transport the press party, it should provide the comfort of a scheduled flight.

The aim in planning the arrangements should be to make the visit as convenient and as comfortable as possible for all those taking part. It should be remembered, for instance, that some people may prefer to come by car, particularly if they wish to go on elsewhere afterwards. Occasionally one hears of press visits which appeared to have been planned more for the convenience of the staff than for those invited to attend! If the press representatives are less than impressed with the arrangements this is likely to be reflected in their reports.

The interest of a visit of this kind is often the opportunity provided for meeting senior executives of the company concerned as much as the actual visit to the works. It is thus a good idea to try to arrange for top management to be well represented. Sometimes senior members of the company travel up with the press, and this is always much appreciated. Apart from this consideration, hospitality demands that the guests should be welcomed at the assembly point by one or more members of staff who will accompany the party and iron out any difficulties that may arise.

A press visit is usually most successful when the party is restricted in number. It is often the practice, therefore, to have a series of press visits on successive days. One day may be allocated to photographers, the next to the national press, radio and television, and the following day to the trade and technical press. This arrangement makes more demands on staff time but it is likely to result in much better coverage.

On many press visits the careful planning is let down by insufficient attention to the choice and briefing of the guides. This is one of the most important parts of the whole operation and it deserves more attention than it sometimes receives.

Even when there are sufficient guides available for the parties to be restricted to six or seven in each, it is still essential for the guides to try to find a quiet spot when they are imparting information. Usually they try to shout against the noise of the machines. This point presents real difficulties, but it should be possible to talk about the machine or process in a quieter spot before coming right into the worst of the din. Where the parties are larger, the whole matter becomes almost impossible: one solution is to install a microphone at one or more vantage points, or for the guides to carry a loud-hailer or simple public address equipment.

The guides should have badges bearing their names so that they may be identified easily. A simple but effective way of allotting the press to their parties should be worked out beforehand; often much time is wasted on what should be a simple manoeuvre, and nothing is more frustrating than milling around waiting to be formed into groups.

When there is a general press visit, the party is a very large one and includes the national press and many branches of the trade and technical press. In such circumstances it is often the practice to group together journalists of like interests when allocating the parties. This results, for example, in all the electrical press representatives finding themselves in the same group. The reasoning behind this is that the guide can be someone qualified to answer difficult or complex questions of an electrical nature. There is, however, a serious snag about this arrangement, since the keen technical journalist is likely to be inhibited in his questioning by the realisation that his closest competitors will also hear the answers—noise of machines permitting.

There are a number of criticisms which apply to many press

facility visits. It is usual and desirable for the managing director, the works manager or some other knowledgeable member of the company to welcome the press, but the speech should be kept short especially when time is limited. There is usually time for a further session of question and answer at the end of the visit, possibly over a cup of tea. Some visits are a positive feat of endurance. The itinerary should be restricted to a reasonable length, especially if much climbing of stairs is involved. It is not a good idea to issue wads of literature which have to be carried round the works; the folder of information can be handed out on the train or aeroplane so that it can be studied in advance and then left in the cloakroom with hats and coats, or it can be issued at the end of the walk.

There will usually be photographs available. The usual practice is to include a few prints in every press folder and to show other photographs, which can be ordered, on a board. It would be a good idea if some attempt was made to give exclusive pictures even on mass visits. This could be achieved if more photographs were taken, even if they were merely taken from a somewhat different angle, and only one print issued of each.

Press arrangements at conferences
Each year there are many luncheons, dinners, meetings and conferences held which are not intended primarily for the press but from which valuable publicity can result if journalists are invited to attend and given facilities for reporting the proceedings. The occasions range from political meetings to annual conferences of learned and scientific bodies. In all instances it is desirable for one responsible official to be given the duty of looking after the press and seeing that they receive—in advance where possible—copies of the programme, agenda and other relevant documents. It is usual for the official's name to be notified to the press in advance so that they know whom to ask for. Whenever possible he should keep himself free of other duties so that he is available to assist the press—for example, by explaining the procedure, identifying speakers, and generally giving any help that the press requires.

It is customary at meetings to provide tables and chairs for the press in a position where they can see and hear clearly. The tables are often immediately in front or at the side of the platform, but in deciding where to place the press it should be borne in mind that they may wish to go out and telephone their stories during the sessions. If adequate telephones are not available nearby, it is necessary to arrange for extra temporary installations. Coin boxes are not required, as, apart from local calls, journalists are accustomed to transfer the charge when speaking to their offices. If the conference lasts more than one day, the journalists will appreciate having a special press room which they can make their headquarters.

When the conference is a highly technical one, it is a good plan to arrange daily briefing meetings for the press at which the chairman or other appropriate official discusses the day's proceedings and is prepared to answer questions. Such meetings help the non-technical journalist to avoid mistakes when writing his reports.

Letters to the editor

A time-honoured and effective way of achieving public notice for a point of view is by using the correspondence columns of newspapers or periodicals. Most editors welcome letters for publication and do not mind the writer expressing partisan views.

Letters to the editor can be grouped into three categories. The letter may comment on a topic of public or private concern; continue an existing correspondence; or comment or complain about a previously published item in the paper. The letter should be composed with care and should be tailored to suit the style of the journal to which it is sent. The style suitable for a letter to a quality newspaper differs appreciably from that appropriate to a tabloid or a weekly.

When a letter is written to correct a mis-statement or ambiguity it is particularly important not to repeat the original error as this will give it a new currency and may bring it to the notice of many readers who may have missed its original publication. This is a point not sufficiently appreciated even by many experienced practitioners.

Judgment should be exercised in deciding the signature of a letter written on behalf of a company or organisation. In general, it is preferable that the letter should be signed by the senior executive most closely concerned with the subject. This is particularly wise when the letter is apologising for inconvenience caused to the public. Such excuses come much better from the chief executive than from the public relations officer.

National newspapers publish only a very small proportion of the letters received. Most provincial newspapers, however, will print any letter which is relevant or of general or local interest.

If a statement which affects the interests of the organisation represented appears in a newspaper or periodical, it is a good plan to telephone the editor, or deputy editor, immediately and to complain in strong terms about the offending item. In most instances of this nature the editor will offer to print a letter putting the opposite point of view and this ensures that the letter will be published when received. It is very rare for papers to publish a correction but most editors will agree to print a letter of explanation even if it is a long and technical one.

In general, of course, letters to the editor should be kept very brief and to the point. If a letter is long it runs the risk of being sub-edited and this may affect some of the main points of the letter. If the subject is an important one it is wise to ask that the letter should not be altered or shortened without the writer's prior agreement.

On matters of general public interest it is possible to secure nationwide publicity by means of letters to the editor if the letters are tailored to suit each publication.

A letter published in a national newspaper will often have very wide repercussions, and the possibility of wide publicity for a letter to the editor is good reason for ensuring that the facts are absolutely true. It is equally essential that the signature of the letter should be genuine. To submit letters for publication under an assumed name is unethical.

Assessing Press Activity
A press office should keep a close watch on everything that appears in the press that has a direct or indirect bearing on the organisation's interests. This will be both to assess the results of any positive press activity carried out and to watch for reports of interest or any which criticise the organisation.

To monitor the whole of the British press is a massive undertaking, and it is usual to subscribe to a press-cutting bureau which undertakes this work for a fee. However, no press-cutting bureau is infallible, and it is often desirable to subscribe to two or more bureaux in order to achieve as complete a coverage as possible. It helps the bureaux to give a good service if they are sent copies of releases issued and are told in advance of special events of particular interest.

In large industries and other organisations which come into daily contact with the public and with public opinion, it is usually considered necessary to monitor the press within the organisation each day.

In a large organisation it is desirable to photocopy press cuttings so that senior executives may receive a file of the actual cuttings to read or browse through. The press office itself should keep records of all press cuttings received, and it is helpful to use the universal decimal system for ease of filing. When there has been a special function, such as the opening of a new building, it is a good plan to stick all the cuttings in a scrap-book, but it is not necessary to go to the extreme of using a gold-blocked leather book. Each cutting should bear the name of the paper, the date, and the position in the paper when it is known.

SUMMARY

There is no obligation on an organisation to have any dealings with the press, but if its activities are of public interest the press will publish reports and comment whether they receive the cooperation of those concerned or not. If they do receive help, there is less likelihood of garbled reports or inaccurate information which can cause embarrassment. In addition, there are many opportunities for securing useful publicity, some of which have been outlined in this chapter.

Even in small organisations, a responsible person should be delegated to act as press officer and to take the trouble to find out how the media works and how an organisation can maintain good relations with the press.

In large organisations, the job of press officer is a full-time responsibility and competent, experienced individuals should be appointed to the position and provided with adequate staff and support.

While press cuttings give an indication of results, they cannot give any reliable quantitative measurement, for the reasons given in Chapter 1.

RADIO AND TELEVISION

The electronic media have entered a period of accelerated change. Rapid development has resulted from the advancements made in photography, in computer and electronic technology, and in satellite transmission.

The result is instantaneous live transmission on a worldwide basis, access to information on a global scale, and technological advancement in receiving systems that are changing the way in which man acquires information.

The rapid changes in technology are having a dramatic effect on the communications industries. Some of these effects are:

1 *Increased specialisation on the part of all mass media.* Magazines, newspapers, radio, and television stations are beginning to recognise that survival is related to fulfilling the needs of specialised interest groups rather than the mass public.

Many stations have narrowed their appeal with the intent of maintaining the support of a special interest group.

2 *Resistance to the change that is inevitable.* The technological change is having dramatic economic repercussions on the print and electronic media.

Television is experiencing the greatest upheaval. Cable television is offering viewers choices never before available. Satellite transmission is increasing the choices and complicating the industry market since stations or cable companies are no longer limited in their viewer range.

3 *The necessity of specialisation and the need for continuing education.* An individual can no longer be a jack of all trades in communications. The public relations professional, in particular, must recognise the need for specialised staff in working with the various media.

Coping with the Changes

Public relations practitioners can best cope with the changes taking place by clearly identifying the specific publics within a society that an organisation needs to reach. When these publics have been identified and analysed through research, then the radio and television stations that best reach the target audiences can be determined and used with effective result.

The practitioner's primary responsibility is to know his target audiences and to ensure that the electronic media selected will reach those audiences. This requires a knowledge of a particular radio or television station's listeners or viewers as well as the listening and viewing habits of the station's audiences in relation to time periods and programming.

Communicating by Television, Radio or Telephone

So far this chapter has been discussing the use of radio and television as media of external communication, but they also provide a most useful tool in the organisation of meetings, press conferences, lectures, etc.

Radio links with other continents are now used regularly, and a similar technique can sometimes usefully be employed in public relations. For example, the chairman's voice can be relayed by radio or telephone private wire to a function in another country when he cannot attend in person. Using the radio or telephone is more effective than employing a record or tape.

Closed-circuit television is no longer a novelty, and is often used at conferences or exhibitions. It has a special use in public relations—for example, in bringing to a shareholders' meeting in London views of a new factory or new processes. By using a large screen for viewing, audiences at meetings or conferences can be shown demonstrations in colour, or black and white, without the necessity and expense of making special films beforehand. Television, moreover, has the sense of immediacy and participation.

BROADCASTING MEDIA OPPORTUNITIES

The opportunities offered by radio and television include:

1 *News bulletins.*

2 *Magazine programmes.*

3 *Interviews, discussion panels, chat shows.*

4 *Current affairs programmes.*

5 *Documentary films.*

6 *Serials and Series.*

Careful study of these programmes will reveal opportunities for securing favourable publicity for their organisations.

TELECONFERENCING

At one time, not so long ago, it was a novelty to think in terms of telephone cable links with other parts of the country or the world to bring messages or speeches from distant parts. Those tentative attempts to provide such links have developed into the modern technology of teleconferencing, video-conferencing or satellite meetings as they are sometimes called.

British Telecom's Confravision from studios was an early example of this kind of distant linkage but the availability of satellite transmission has greatly increased the possibilities of this kind of linking together distant participants.

Teleconferencing is more suited to use by large companies, finding it organisationally and cost-effective to employ this as an alternative to travel by their managers, than for conference use. It should be remembered, however, that some particularly large scale or prestigious events may lend themselves to this modern method of linkage.

A striking example of the successful use of this new technique was at a conference called 'Gastrolink'. This featured an endoscope operation performed in London and witnessed by a medical team in New York as well as a huge audience in the UK and Ireland. During the operation viewers could talk directly to the consultant while he worked and a running commentary was given by a doctor via an audio and video link from the Portman Hotel in London where the Gastrolink symposium was taking place.

It is reported that this event required three satellite links, two microwave links, seven direct audio links, 163 telephone lines, 105 satellite receivers and a back-up staff of 200, supported by 400 technical people. This expensive operation was judged a very cost-effective way of reaching such a vast and important audience.

British Telecom and its European counterparts are making similar facilities available in London, Rome, Paris and Frankfurt. Interactive teleconferencing by satellite is now available for any event which requires such linkage and can justify the cost.

It was reported in *The Times* of 6 September 1988 that British Government departments are now making extensive use of video-conferencing and are now Britain's largest single user of this technique which allows group meetings to take place over a video link-up. Other British companies making extensive use of this method include BP, British Gas, Ford, STC, Barclays Bank and IBM.

4   *The printed word*

The printed word is likely to remain the most important medium of communication between any organisation and the outside world. Television has increased the demand for books and reading material of all kinds instead of reducing it. Media relations has been dealt with in Chapter 3, but there remains the great variety of printed material which an organisation produces for both internal and external use.

The printed matter will include office forms, invoices, letterheadings and items of this nature which have little relevance to public relations, except that there is a great deal to be said for adopting a uniform house style. A large organisation may have a stationery department to order the various kinds of office printing, but the public relations staff should be given the opportunity of making suggestions on the style and design of all these printed items. In a smaller organisation it is most desirable that all printed matter should be a public relations responsibility.

Style and Design
To look at a magazine published some years ago is to notice the great changes that have occurred in the choice of type faces and the style of illustrations. This is particularly striking in the case of the advertisements, which often lead the way in design. One becomes accustomed to contemporary print design from advertising seen on all sides and from packaging design, and it is a fallacy to think that

the average man or woman is not influenced by the appearance of printed matter. Japan now regards presentation as a particularly potent trade weapon.

Many organisations have adopted a house style which has become so well known that their products or advertisements are recognised instantly. The house style may consist of a logotype, or a particular typeface, or a special colour, or a combination of these factors. A house style is used to good effect by most international organisations.

A well-designed house style will lend itself to modification so that it can be used effectively on items differing as widely as letterheadings and delivery vans. If an organisation publishes a wide variety of items including company reports, house journals, catalogues and reference books, it would be inappropriate for all these publications to have the same typography or cover design, but there is much to be gained from having a recognisable family relationship common to all publications.

The design of print is only one example of how it is possible to project the character of an organisation in such a way that it is readily recognisable by the public. The intelligent use of good design in everything an organisation does—its buildings, its products, its public behaviour, etc—can do much to secure public approval.

In the international sphere, and particularly in relation to overseas telephone usage, it is important not to ignore pronunciations when selecting initials or other devices for product identities.

Knowing about Typography
It is not essential for those in public relations to possess an expert knowledge of typography, but it is vital to believe that typography matters. In simple words it means the organisation of the printed word and its effect on the reader. It is obvious that the success of the printed word will depend on the success of its typography. As in other branches of craftsmanship, taste will vary considerably and it may be difficult to secure agreement on what is *good* typography; but there should be less difficulty in recognising and extirpating *bad* typography. Here again, however, taste varies with time and with geographical location, and it would be wrong for the public relations adviser to try to ride roughshod over the likes and dislikes of his management. Rather it is his duty to educate and to interest others in

typography, and thus to obtain the opportunity to make experiments in the use of print.

Only organisations that produce a very great number of publications can afford to have their own typographer, so it is customary to use the services of a freelance graphic designer. Often one uses several different designers to achieve a greater variety of ideas. An experienced typographer is an expert in graphic design, but an experienced public relations practitioner knows the effect he is trying to achieve and should not be afraid of backing his own opinion during design discussions.

A number of specialist companies have sprung up which offer an advisory and publishing service in rather the same way that a film producing company makes films. If they are fully briefed on the object of the publication, the readers to whom it is addressed, the budget, etc, they will prepare suggestions and, when these are approved, carry through the production right to the final delivery whether it is a publicity leaflet, a prestige booklet or a history of the firm. Some of these companies do excellent work, and this method of dealing with publications is to be recommended in those cases where the public relations department is too small to handle its own print.

Working with the Printer
Public relations brings one into constant contact with printers, and although practical experience of printing is not necessary it is essential to have a good working knowledge of printing processes and methods and some knowledge of the jargon. Without this background knowledge one cannot argue with the printer, or assess critically the advice of typographers whose enthusiasm sometimes may run away with them, without due regard for what is practicable or economic.

There are many good books on the history and practice of printing, and most printers will be willing to show you round their works. Visiting a number of different print works is one of the best ways of acquiring a basic knowledge of printing, and these visits give an opportunity of making a critical appraisal of the manner in which the various printers organise their works. There is no doubt that printers prefer to work with clients who know something about the craft, but it is foolish to try to hoodwink them pretending to know more than one actually does.

There are three main factors in obtaining printing services: cost, service, and quality of the finished work. As in most things, one tends to get the quality of printing for which one is prepared to pay. Printers fall into different price categories based on the degree of service they can offer the customer. The best printers provide a typographical and design service, an extremely wide range of type faces, a high standard of proof-reading, and do everything possible to make printing effortless for the customer. A printer in one of the lowest price categories, however, does not have any proof-readers—the foreman does what reading there is—and the client has to exercise the utmost care to ensure that the final result is satisfactory. Between these extremes there is every variety, and the secret is to find a printer whose service and standards are high but whose prices are reasonable.

The quality of original 'copy', photographs or line drawings sent for reproduction is vitally important. Generally speaking, no printed result can be better than the originals. If 'touching-up' is required, this should be done before the work reaches the printer as this is not regarded as a proper element of the printing function.

Corrections on proofs should be very clearly marked, preferably with a coloured ball-point pen—never in pencil!

Service covers a number of points. It is desirable to be able to contact the printer quickly, and where a printing works is remote it is essential to have an efficient town office to deal with. A printer plans his work in rotation, but should be willing to work overtime to print some item that is wanted urgently. Keeping to time is not one of the natural virtues of most printers, but one is entitled to expect that a printer will give a time schedule for a job and keep to it provided he receives the copy on time and there is no undue delay in passing proofs.

A well-conceived publication can fail in its object if it is poorly printed or contains typographical errors. For this reason it is usually false economy in public relations to seek the lowest price for print. The practice of inviting tenders for *every* print job is not to be recommended, for it puts unnecessary work on printers' estimating departments and interferes with the establishment of a continuing connection with a printer which enables him to provide the best service. One would always invite tenders for printing a new house journal or regular publication of that kind, but for jobbing printing it is wiser to know one's printer and to trust him to charge a fair price. The ideal arrangement is to use three or four printers, choosing the one most suitable for each particular job. When the staff at the works know you, they will usually put that little extra effort into the work they are doing for you that will ensure a first-class result.

There can be no condoning of bad printing. Advance copies of any publication should be inspected, and if there are any serious errors or blemishes they should be put right before the job is issued even if it means reprinting some of the pages. If the printer is responsible for the errors there would not be any extra charge. Even if it means paying extra, every effort should be made to achieve a perfect result if the publication is an important one. To have to include an *erratum* slip in a publication is an admission of incompetence.

The greatest extravagance in printing is to change one's mind at the proof stage. Once proofs have been submitted it can cost a great deal to meet second thoughts, and this point should be emphasised at every opportunity. Unfortunately, some of those in authority do not seem capable of knowing what they wish to say until they see it actually in print, and many people are unable to resist the temptation to alter a proof. These last-minute changes are costly and may jeopardise the delivery date.

It is necessary to watch very carefully charges made by some printers for 'authors' corrections'. A printer should be prepared to justify these charges.

The most successful printing job will not necessarily be the one that was printed regardless of cost. In fact it is as much a solecism to over-dress a publication as it is to over-dress oneself. The style and quality of a publication should be chosen so that it is in keeping with the function that it is intended to perform.

Keeping Abreast of Modern Printing Methods
Letterpress was the generally accepted method of printing for over five hundred years, but its supremacy has been supplanted by photogravure and offset lithography.

Linocuts and woodcuts are other examples of the relief method which is the basis of letterpress. The type or printing stereos and blocks are raised above the surface and receive the printing ink which is transferred to the paper. Letterpress gives a crisp, clear impression, the type can be set by machine and any necessary corrections are easily made and inserted making it the method of choice for all printing containing a considerable amount of text. Modern developments in letterpress have included the introduction of the electronic scanning method of making blocks and the introduction of photo-typesetting which takes the place of metal type.

In photogravure the process is an intaglio one, ie the printing areas are below the non-printing areas, as in engraving and etching processes. The ink fills the recesses in the surface, and as the printing takes place the ink is sucked up out of the recess on to the paper giving opacity, depth of colour and a fine tonal range.

Lithography is a planographic process, ie the printing surface is flat. The printing areas are treated so that they accept the ink, while the non-printing areas of the surface reject the ink. Lithography is based on the principles that grease and water do not mix. There is no relief surface to give a sharp edge to the ink, so the result usually has a typical softness and a slightly restricted tonal range.

Photogravure and lithography are particularly suitable for colour printing, (but are only an economic proposition if the runs are substantial.)

Screen process printing is a stencil type of operation and was originally known as silk screen printing. This term is no longer accurate, as silk bolting cloth is not the only material used now. Ink is squeezed through the openings of a selectively blocked-out fabric, and an amazing variety of different inks can be employed in this type of printing. Screen printing is used extensively for posters, printing on to metal and other materials, and for printing textiles and wallpapers.

The popularity of office offset machines is being replaced by desk top production techniques. Where there is a considerable amount of office printing to be done, such as forms, internal memoranda, or information booklets, the installation of an office offset machine is an economic proposition, and it provides facilities for printing more ambitious items very quickly when the occasion demands. There are many different kinds of office offset machines on the market, and some of the more elaborate models can do excellent printing. Many printers have installed them in their own works for doing certain types of work but only if they expect to have sufficient work for these machines to justify the capital outlay.

The term 'web offset' in printing can be defined as a process which transfers an image from a rubber blanket on to a continuous web (reel) of paper. This development of the lithographic process has established itself during recent years and has replaced letterpress and rotary machines for the printing of many magazines and newspapers. It provides high-speed printing of good quality, in monochrome or colour.

Computer photo-typesetting is making steady progress and is particularly suitable for directories or year-books, as it is easy to update the text each year and to incorporate alterations and additions. Its extension to general printing has been slower, but computer typesetting is used successfully by a number of newspapers.

Desk Top Publishing
The introduction of personal computers into normal office routine has brought with it the possibility of printing in-house a wide range of items and achieving good definition. This facility is replacing the widespread use of small office printing machines.

The essential equipment required is a powerful computer, a monitor, a scanner and a good printer, preferably a laser printer. Then, using appropriate software packages, high definition print can be produced, with a wide variety of type sizes and fonts and layout possibilities.

The production of newsletters, brochures, leaflets, office stationery and even annual reports can be achieved but the results are likely to be disappointing unless the operator has considerable typographical and design skills, coupled with familiarity and experience with the equipment.

For most of us, the use of photo-typesetting and professional printing will continue to be the best option.

Printing Paper
The choice of the right paper is important in securing a first-class result. The paper should be chosen in the light of the desired effect. In certain types of publication a rough paper or a cartridge paper may be much more effective than a coated or art paper. If you buy your paper direct, the paper merchant's representative will be glad to advise you on the selection of paper; but also discuss the question with your printer, as he has to print on the paper!

It is a good idea to have a specimen page proofed on different types of paper before making the final choice. It can be very difficult to match the exact house style colour when using different types of printing papers.

Paper is made in a number of standard sizes, and to have special sizes made is a costly procedure. It is desirable to bear this point in mind when planning a publication. The ideal is to have a paper size that permits illustrations to 'bleed' but does not leave much paper to be cut off when trimming to size.

The 'International Paper Sizes'—the 'A' sizes—have become generally accepted. Whether an organisation adopts these standard sizes or not, it is wise to select a few standard sizes and to keep to them for all publications. A4 format, is very suitable for magazines and house journals. A5—ie half A4—is very convenient for small leaflets or brochures (A4 is 297 mm x 210 mm).

The weight of paper, measured in grammes per square metre (gsm), should be considered, particularly for end products to be mailed, or air mailed.

House Journals

One of the well-established media of public relations is the house journal. This title is to be preferred to the older 'house magazine', even though the purist will point out that few if any house journals are published daily!

The value of house journals in promoting good public relations, both internally and externally, is demonstrated by the rapid increase in the numbers published. In the United Kingdom there are more than 1800 house journals with a circulation of over 23 million published at an annual production cost of nearly £15 million. In the USA there are said to be ten thousand house journals with a circulation of three hundred million, in Japan about three thousand journals, and in France seven hundred.

The usual definition of a house journal is that it is a non-profit-making periodical publication published by an organisation to maintain contact with its employees or with the public. House journals vary in size, style and type so greatly that it is usual to classify them by their readership. They are either published for internal readership, for external distribution, or for a combination of the two.

'Internals' may be intended for all an organisation's employees, or for certain factories or other specialised groups. 'Externals' may be general prestige publications, or directed at specific sections of the public, customers, dealers, etc. It is almost impossible to pin-point the readership of the dual-purpose house journal, and this is a serious weakness of this type of publication. Moreover the two different purposes usually call for different treatment.

There is a tendency for some editors of house journals to consider they are performing a function which is outside the public relations programme of the organisation. It is true that an internal house journal plays an important part in personnel relations, but many aspects of public relations impinge on the field of personnel relations and in all large organisations there is a constant need for close liaison between those working in these allied fields.

In a large organisation, the editor of the house journal is likely to be engaged full time on this work; but in smaller companies, or where the house journal appears quarterly or even less frequently, it is likely to be the responsibility of the public relations department. There is no reason why this arrangement should not work satisfactorily, and there is little foundation in the suggestion that if a public relations executive edits the internal house journal he is likely to forget the importance of giving adequate attention to 'hatched, matched and dispatched' information in favour of catering for outside readers. Above all, the job of editor should never be given to a person without previous experience or training.

A journal inevitably reflects the personality of the editor, and if the editor is the right man he—or she—should be allowed to get on with the job. The right time to criticise is after an issue has appeared, when comments and views are useful in helping to shape future issues. It has never been possible to edit successfully by committee, and it never will produce a successful result. The classic example was the editor of a house journal who had to report to a works committee of thirty-two persons. Each article had to be read out in full, before publication, to this committee, who took the opportunity of criticising nearly every word. Fortunately for the sanity of the editor in question, a different method was adopted later!

Generalisations are notoriously misleading, and this is particularly true when considering house journals. No two journals have the same background, and the aims and objects vary considerably according to the circumstances of the organisation. In the case of 'internals' there are a number of controversial points which arouse heated discussion. Should employees pay for the house journal, and if so how much? Should the journal be issued at the works, or should it be sent to the homes of employees? Should payment be made to employees who contribute articles or items of news? Should advertising be accepted? Should each issue include a policy statement from the chief executive? To what extent should humour—and pin-ups—be allowed? These are a few of the questions which have to be decided when planning an internal house journal; but there are no ready-made answers, for many variants have proved equally successful.

It is always helpful if the editor has a knowledge of printing processes used in producing his journal. Most printers would be happy to give a loyal customer the benefit of a condensed 'course' on basic principles and problems in his works.

The main purpose of an employee journal is to foster a family feeling by taking the workers and staff into the confidence of management, explaining policies, and seeking their interest and cooperation. This would make a dull journal—however cleverly it was interpreted—unless it were supplemented by more general reading and by a full coverage of staff activities. House journals present wonderful opportunities for imaginative editing, hampered only by the need usually to keep within a fairly tight budget, and it is a pity that so few editors rise fully to the occasion. The best internal house journals are excellent, but the general standard is still mediocre.

The majority of employee journals are booklet size, but a few have used the newspaper format very successfully. Where the print order is fairly large and the main object of the journal is the provision of news and information, the newspaper style is preferable and probably has more impact.

When a house journal has become established, the management often thinks it would like to send complimentary copies to local functionaries, to customers, and to others who come into regular contact with the organisation. Provided the standard of the journal is high, there is no reason why this wider distribution should not be permitted. The danger, however, is that the fact of this wide distribution may lead to the editor receiving instructions to modify the editorial policy. This leads to a vain attempt to satisfy two different types of readership, and usually to a deterioration in the standard of the journal.

Some internal-external journals have proved successful, but usually when the difficulties inherent in this type of journal have been faced squarely from the outset. It must be recognised that it is far better to have separate house journals to meet the needs of the internal and external readership. Apart from editorial aspects, it is wasteful to produce an internal journal to the *de luxe* standards suitable for a prestige publication, and in fact such lavishness might arouse resentment from the unions. It is likely to prove cheaper to have two separate journals than to publish an internal-external journal.

The external prestige house journal is approaching very near to the commercial periodical publishing field, and is in fact an example of a controlled circulation magazine—but published to promote public relations rather than to attract advertising support.

There has been a steady improvement in house journal design and editing. One still meets, however, examples that are so bad that they must have an adverse effect on the sponsor's reputation.

Despite the growing importance of television and radio, it is certain that the printed word will continue to be a very important medium of public relations.

Direct Mail
Leaflets, pamphlets broadsheets, letters and telegrams have often had a profound effect, and have at times changed the course of history. They remain a very effective medium of communication and often find a place in a public relations campaign.

It may be a question of sending out a few dozen letters, or several thousand, but the principles are the same. The letter must appear to be a personal communication, and the recipient must feel that it has a message for him. The wording should be to the point and free from ambiguity. The letter may be printed by one of the methods which closely resemble the effect of typewriting, but it should be addressed to the person for whom it is intended and signed individually. A letter with a printed or rubber-stamped signature loses any possibility of being regarded as a personal communication. A letter sent to a medium or large company is unlikely to reach a suitable recipient unless it has the correct name and title of the addressee on it.

At one time, the personalisation of direct mail letters, in which the recipient is addressed by name, was most impressive but this facility has been used so much by *Readers Digest* and many large advertisers that it has lost its magic.

Opinion is divided as to whether better results are obtained from a very short letter—on one side of the sheet—or from a longer letter which can give more information and thus arouse a greater degree of interest. There is agreement, however, that it is always desirable to follow up the first communication by others if anything useful is to be achieved.

It is always wise to make it easy for the recipient to do what is requested. More replies can be expected if it is only a matter of making a few ticks on a questionnaire, and if an addressed or prepaid envelope is enclosed, than if it is necessary to write a letter in reply.

Direct mail advertising has been developed to a high degree, and many of the techniques can be adopted when communicating through the post for public relations purposes.

5 Photography in public relations

In the chapter dealing with press relations comments were made on the provision of photographs for the press at conferences and on facility visits. The use of photography in public relations deserves special attention, as many people do not realise the full potentialities of photographs.

The first point to appreciate is that photographs always lend authenticity. One knows that photographs can be as misleading as statistics, but nevertheless they are generally accepted as authentic proof of facts or events.

Good photographs have a compelling appeal that is absent from printed matter, however well laid out and displayed. Few publications are found these days in which photographs and other types of illustrations are absent, for it has become generally accepted that photographs add to the interest and stimulate attention. This is now true even of companies' annual reports, which were formerly austere documents but are now usually illustrated.

Quality of Photography
The word 'good' used in the opening sentence of the last paragraph is very important. As photographs have become accepted as a suitable embellishment to all types of printed matter, the reading public has become more critical of the quality of photographs and the skill with which they are presented. Fortunately, improved types of film and better understanding of camera techniques and printing

methods have resulted in very much better results being achieved by professional photographers. A closer study of technique and lighting, and the wide development of photography in industry, have attracted a much higher standard of entrant to the profession.

Public relations practitioners should demand a very high standard from the photographers they use, and not be content with anything less. Just as a good photograph enhances a story, so does a poor one depreciate its effect. In certain instances where it is essential to use a photograph, and it is not possible to try again, recourse may be made to retouching—but this should only be done as a last resort, as retouching tends to give an artificial look.

Uses of Photographs

1 To illustrate news stories which are to appear in newspapers or the technical press.

2 To illustrate reports, booklets, house journals, etc.

3 For record purposes.

4 For use in advertisements or posters.

5 For training and research.

Advertising photography is outside the scope of this book. Some of the results achieved in this field are works of art; even today, however, some photographs used in advertisements are poor in quality. Photographs for record purposes are very important, but present little technical difficulty since the purpose is to achieve an exact likeness. Photographs for news purposes or for use in publications are another matter: here there is endless opportunity for ingenuity and art.

Photography at Special Events

The most effective way to achieve editorial picture publicity for an event such as an exhibition, an opening of a building, or a conference, is to issue a general invitation to the photographic agencies and to the press. It is often desirable to invite photographers to attend earlier than the general press preview as this photo call gives them better opportunities. They will probably wish to attend the official opening as well.

In the United Kingdom, royal occasions and other special events bring into operation the 'rota system'. A limited number of passes are issued: to representatives of the national press—through the Newspaper Proprietors' Association; to the provincial press—through the Newspaper Society; and to the photographic press agencies—through the Council of Photographic News Agencies. Photographs taken by the 'rota' photographers are made available to all newspapers and agencies.

In countries where a rota system is not in operation the results can be chaotic.

When organising an event, it is usually wise to arrange with a photographer or agency to cover it fully for the organisers rather than to rely on results of photographers who might attend. This method also takes care of the copyright problem, for if you commission and pay for the photographs you can then use them in any way you wish.

Photographs as News Stories
The press will often use photographs which tell a story, eg the chief executive leaving on a trip to Moscow, a very large piece of equipment being shipped overseas, a presentation to a worker who has completed fifty years' service, foreign engineers visiting a factory, etc. The essential points are:

1 They must be striking and interesting photographs.

2 They must be topical.

3 They must be adequately captioned.

4 Every picture should tell a story; if in addition it is pleasing aesthetically, the value is increased.

Photographs of this kind provide very useful editorial publicity, and often one photograph appears in a great variety of publications at home and overseas. It is noticeable that some organisations achieve much more success in this field than other equally important companies. The answer is to be found in the relative quality of the prints submitted. Sometimes, however, excellent prints arrive in editorial offices in poor condition owing to failure to protect them properly. Prints are often spoilt by unwise use of paper clips or by writing on the reverse side with a ball-point pen or hard pencil.

Photographs for Publications

When photographs are needed for publications, it is possible to plan ahead and thus to achieve better results than are always possible in the case of photographs of news events where immediacy is the first essential. The industrial photographer is able to illustrate not only what is going on in industry, but also something of its life and spirit. This is creative art, and there are many fine photographers who are achieving results which can be used to great effect in a public relations programme. Some of these photographs, in colour or monochrome, can be used very effectively on stands at exhibitions and trade fairs in the form of very large transparencies or prints, and these can also be used for display purposes. Sometimes it is possible to get good results in black and white when colour is impracticable.

The best industrial photographers take their work very seriously and like to have adequate time to plan their pictures. It is unrealistic to expect a photographer to walk into a factory and to be able to decide immediately on the pictures that will best express the spirit of the place. A good photographer will be able to achieve results on the spur of the moment, but he will undoubtedly achieve better pictures if he has the time to look around and to plan a series of pictures that will tell the story to the best advantage. This will involve not only a study of the appearance of different parts of the plant, but also talking to some of the personnel and trying to understand something of the living tradition of the job.

Many pictures will include a person or some familiar object in order to give an idea of the true size. This often introduces difficulties. The people photographed quite naturally wish to look their best, and if allowed to do so will put on clothes or headgear out of keeping with the situation. One sometimes sees photographs of men working lathes, wearing ties because presumably they or the photographer thought they looked smarter. The result looks incongruous, and it would be against the Factories Act as well! It is equally wrong to photograph men wearing spotless white overalls operating large machines. The use of white overalls should be reserved for people you would expect to see dressed in this way, such as inspectors, or men and women working under 'clean' or hygienic conditions.

In black and white photography the effect depends mainly on the dramatic use of light and shade. It is the artistic use of lighting that gives a picture its hidden power.

Most top-rank industrial photographers insist on printing their own photographs so that they may control the quality which can make or mar the result of their work with the camera. This is a desire with which the customer should have every sympathy. Using really qualified and competent professional photographers is fairly expensive, but using those whose results cannot be published with pride is often more costly.

Many companies employ their own photographers, and some of them achieve excellent results. Too often, however, the staff photographer is inadequately paid and grossly overworked. He is sometimes expected to do all the clerical and administrative work in addition to operating the dark-room and taking all the photographs. If a concern is large enough to need its own staff photographer, it should be prepared to budget for adequate professional and supporting staff.

Staff photographers should be given every encouragement to do good work and to improve their skill. No public relations department can afford to have a poor photographer on its staff, but a person showing promise of making a good photographer should be given every opportunity of realising their potential.

Questions of Copyright
It is necessary to consider the copyright of photographs used for different purposes in public relations.

1   Copyright in photographs specifically commissioned from a photographer belongs to the client.

2   Copyright in photographs taken by a photographer and subsequently offered to and accepted by a client remains that of the photographer.

3   Unless otherwise negotiated, negatives are normally retained by the photographer.

Photographs issued to the media can normally be used without fee. This fact is normally stated on the back of prints.

When using live models, ensure that they complete the 'standard form for signature by models', devised by the Institute of Incorporated Photographers and the Institute of Practitioners in Advertising.

Storage of Prints and Negatives

Prints and negatives are a valuable asset and deserve a good filing and retrieval system.

Whatever system is adopted, it should be possible to locate prints or negatives quickly. The system should detail the type of negative or print and if there are any restrictions on use.

Photographic Libraries

In some instances it is more satisfactory to obtain a photograph from a photographic library than to endeavour to have pictures taken specially. This is, of course, essential when dealing with events that are past history. Fortunately there is a wide variety of libraries which can supply photographs on almost every subject.

Most large industrial companies run their own photographic libraries, and will usually be very willing to supply prints for use by other people subject to suitable acknowledgment. In some cases they will even take photographs specially to meet requests.

Finally, mention should be made of the photographic libraries of newspapers and many periodicals. They are excellent when exclusivity is not essential.

Securing the Best Results from Photography

There are six main points to watch:

1 Secure the best photographer for the particular type of assignment. It is more useful to have a few photographs by an expert than many by a less brilliant exponent.

2 Give the photographer a careful briefing on the type of photographs required. It is necessary to tell him what subjects to cover, but the best results will come from giving him a fairly free hand. He will often obtain striking and original results, even from most unpromising material.

3 Make sure that he has every facility for getting good results. Make sure that the factory manager knows that the photographer is coming, and why the photographs are needed, in order to secure his willing rather than grudging cooperation. Always go with the photographer yourself, or send a senior colleague, in order to ensure that the photographer is allowed all the time that he regards as necessary to get good results.

4   Ensure that all prints and negatives are adequately housed and catalogued for easy reference. When issuing photographs, always see that each print has a reference number and that it is adequately captioned. The caption should include the vital facts—who, where, why, or when—and as much additional information as possible. There is no need for the caption to be brief. The editor using the photograph will prefer to write his own short caption from the full details you supply. Attach the caption to the back of the photograph so that it hangs down in front of the print.

5   When using photographs yourself for reproduction, take considerable trouble to ensure the best result by 'cropping' the print. This may be in order to alter the proportions of the photograph, eg to fit a front cover, or to eliminate a blemish or extraneous object, or to concentrate attention on a particular section of the photograph. Intelligent cropping of a photograph can work wonders. Sometimes it is helpful to consult the photographer about the trimming of a print for he may have a little more on the negative; and with his knowledge of composition he can possibly help to suggest the most effective manner of making the reproduction.

6   Carefully examine prints before use, in order to make sure that there are no old tin cans, trailing wires or other accidental and unwanted extras in the picture. If any blemishes of this kind cannot be eliminated by cropping the picture, recourse has to be had to retouching.

6 Exhibitions and Trade Fairs*

Modern exhibition and trade fairs have become an accepted medium of public relations and marketing. There is no clear demarcation between an exhibition and a trade fair, and the terms are interchanged freely. A trade fair, however, as its name implies, is staged for the purpose of selling goods or demonstrating new ideas and techniques. An exhibition, on the other hand, may range from a prestige international show, like the 1988 Brisbane World Fair, to small educational displays in a local public library or factory canteen.

Trade fairs are not really within the scope of this book, but their organisation and control are very similar to those of a public relations exhibition. Furthermore, in most organisations the public relations department would be responsible for all types of exhibitions so the subject of exhibiting will be discussed in general terms.*

Exhibiting breaks down into these three fairly clear-cut sections:

1   Deciding which exhibitions to support, and to what degree.

2   Preparing a brief, and organising the construction of the stand.

3   Staffing and controlling the stand during the duration of

---

*The subject of this chapter is dealt with in greater detail in 'Exhibitions and Conferences from A to Z' by Professor Sam Black ISBN 0 903629 02X published by Modino Press 1989.

the exhibition. This will include the period prior to the opening and during the dismantling.

Choosing the Exhibitions to Support

Hundreds of exhibitions take place every year, at home and overseas, and it is very difficult to decide which of these should be supported. In any industry certain exhibitions will be considered as obvious ones to support, but beyond these there is considerable scope for making the right or wrong choice.

In many instances, the decision to support a particular exhibition may be taken by the chief executive or by the board; but the public relations adviser should be asked for an opinion, and he should be competent to express a useful view on a question which is likely to involve considerable expenditure. It is difficult to judge an exhibition without having visited it at least once, and therefore every opportunity should be taken of going to exhibitions and trade fairs at home and overseas. It is often misleading to assess the value of an exhibition from secondhand information.

There are several points on which information is needed. It is desirable to know the exact scope of the exhibition, the size of the attendance, and the type of visitors it attracts. It is necessary to form an assessment of the merits of overseas exhibitions relative to other exhibitions of a similar or allied type in the same country or continent. Knowledge of the exhibiting conditions in an overseas exhibition will be useful in giving an idea of the expense likely to be involved.

In considering whether to support a particular trade fair, it is likely that the marketing department will have submitted their views on the sales likely to result from participation. There will thus be factual data on which to form a decision. It is more difficult to assess the likely value of a prestige or public relations exhibit, and the decision is likely to be taken on opinions rather than on hard facts. In considering the question, it should be borne in mind that a stand in an exhibition can be supported by a number of other public relations activities. Another point that often influences a decision to exhibit is the negative view that the company or organisation cannot afford to be missing when others are present in strength.

Thought should be given to whether the timing of the exhibition is convenient in respect of production programmes, and whether it clashes with similar exhibitions taking place elsewhere.

The next question that arises is how much space is needed to display adequately the articles or services that are to be exhibited. Here the question of cost comes into the reckoning for, except in the case of small stands, the cost is more or less proportional to the floor space. A further complication is that in certain exhibitions it is necessary to reserve a large space in order to get an 'island' site or a position on the ground floor. It is also necessary in some instances to exhibit regularly in order to maintain a good place in the ballot for stand allocation.

Budget for Stands
It is usual to reckon the cost of exhibiting as £x per square metre of net stand space. This figure covers the total cost of constructing the stand, and includes the fees to designers. It does not include the floor rent or staff costs, insurance and carriage. These latter items will be very heavy indeed if the exhibition is in Moscow, New York, Peking, or other distant situation.

Considerable variation is possible in the amount spent on the construction of the stand, although prestige exhibits usually deserve *de luxe* treatment whereas trade stands can often be simpler or may be part of a 'shell' scheme—standard units provided by the organisers. The practice of 'keeping up with the Joneses' has tended to inflate exhibition costs unnecessarily at some exhibitions where the subject is of a technical nature and excessive elaboration is out of character.

As an approximation, a stand could work out at about £500 per square metre, but a large stand featuring heavy machinery at an engineering exhibition might cost as little as £200 per square metre.

In addition to the basic costs, there are many opportunities for elaboration—all of which will increase the cost. In general, it is not worth embarking on a prestige exhibit, either at home or overseas, unless the money is available to do the job well. Naturally a double-decker stand will cost more per square metre; and when an improvised structure is used, or a special building is constructed, the costs may rocket. Labour costs are always a high proportion of an overseas exhibition budget, which is why prefabricated units can be very useful.

It is essential to draw up a careful budget and to do everything possible to keep the cost of each item within its allotted sum. It is usual to allow a substantial sum, say ten per cent, to cover contingencies.

Mobile Exhibits
The usual procedure in exhibition work is for the contractor to construct the stand, lending the materials for the duration of the show and then returning all usable parts to his general store. This does not apply to models, photographs, transparencies, etc, which can be used again possibly at future exhibitions. This method of construction is undoubtedly the most satisfactory way of working, but laymen on committees constantly query the idea. The popular idea is that it should be possible to design and construct an exhibition stand which can then be used over and over again at different shows. This would be a practical proposition if all stands were the same shape and size. Furthermore, stands are usually built of fairly lightweight materials which stand up to a short life but would not survive removal to other sites without extensive repair and renovation. Few organisations, too, have the storage space necessary, and if storage is hired it has to be paid for.

The ideal is that each stand should be designed to fit the actual site and to take advantage of all the circumstances. A mobile stand would not be so adaptable, and would have to be built of stouter materials in the first place. In short, the snags usually outweigh the possible advantages. It is, of course, quite practical to make sections of a stand that can be used at different exhibitions, but it is not a good idea to try to transport the whole stand or the major part of it. The one exception is when a small travelling exhibition is planned. Such a show will usually be staged in an empty room or hall, and it is possible to design a series of displays which can be erected to form exhibitions of different sizes and shapes according to the venue.

Travelling exhibitions will fail unless they are simple to erect and do not require the services of a dozen men and a team of electricians. The components of the exhibition must be strong enough to stand up to the rigours of frequent transport, but light enough to avoid heavy carriage and labour costs.

Organising the Stand
Enough has been said to indicate the problems involved in making the correct decisions on whether to exhibit in any particular

exhibition. The need is to have a clear idea of what it is hoped to achieve from exhibiting in a specific show, and to make an objective assessment of the likelihood of achieving these aims at an economic cost. This is the ideal; too often the decision is made in response to an impassioned appeal from the organiser, or because the competitors will all be there.

Having decided to exhibit in a certain exhibition, there is need for clear thinking about the form the exhibit should take. In general, exhibition techniques are most successful when they are used to portray solid objects, or ideas which lend themselves to three-dimensional representation. Photographs, diagrams, illustrations and text can be used effectively to support a three-dimensional presentation, but they lack sufficient interest-catching ability if used alone. Models are used a great deal nowadays, and some of them are very fine works with every part moving. A stand that is entirely made up of models, however, may give an impression of miniaturisation: so where models are employed, it is desirable to have some objects that are life-size to give the right idea of scale. Another possible weakness is when models are made to different scales. It is a good plan to work to a common scale of, say, one-quarter of life-size when a number of models are likely to be used together on one stand.

Animated flow diagrams, recorded sound, telephones giving messages in a number of languages, murals, sculptures and many other novelties are used by designers to give exhibition stands that 'little extra something the others haven't got'. These cannot make an exhibit successful, however, if there is not an idea to put over which lends itself to three-dimensional treatment.

The Brief
The first step is to consult all the interests involved and to ascertain their requirements in order that a comprehensive brief can be drawn up. 'Brief' may be a quite inappropriate word for the voluminous document which may be necessary to include all the items required. An exhibition stand, however, unless it is a very large one, cannot possibly portray a very great number of different ideas, and the brief may have to be pruned before it can be interpreted satisfactorily.

Designing the Stand
Unless an organisation has its own exhibition design staff, it is necessary either to appoint a contractor who provides a design

service, or to engage the services of a specialist architect-designer. The former method is not ideal unless the contractor has a very high reputation for attention to design. Furthermore it interferes with the customary method of putting the approved designs out to tender. The designer has to be paid for his work, of course, whether it is met by the client directly or indirectly.

Fees are usually worked out on a sliding scale as a proportion of the total construction costs supervised by the designer. The scale varies from twenty per cent of a small budget to ten per cent on a really big job. These are average fees, and a higher fee will be justified if the brief is a particularly complex one or if much travelling is involved.

The designer will study the brief, and may wish to visit the organisation's offices and works and to talk to some of the staff in order to obtain the feel of the organisation's aims and policies. In due course the designer will present preliminary ideas which will eventually become the agreed plan of the stand. The process of reaching agreement with the designer is likely to be easier if he has been chosen in the knowledge of his type of approach to the problem. Most exhibition designers will tackle any type of stand; but some are more successful with particular subjects, and the public relations adviser is likely to be more in sympathy with the techniques of certain of the designers. It is, therefore, wise to make a point of finding out which designers have been responsible for the various main stands at exhibitions visited.

If the brief presented to the designer was adequate, he should have been able to prepare an acceptable scheme for the stand, bearing in mind the position of the stand in the exhibition hall and the natural features such as light and balconies. Unless a designer is thoroughly familiar with the exhibition hall in question, it is most desirable that he should visit the site before the plans are finalised. On one occasion, when this was not done, a stand at a trade fair had to be reorganised on the site to make the best of the natural light from a large glass roof. A study of the plans is not always an adequate substitute for a visit to the site.

When the stand is a large or complicated one, it is a good idea to ask the designer to supply a small scale model. This will give a clear impression of the details of the finished stand, and will be very useful when discussing the stand with members of the organisation unaccustomed to visualising drawings in terms of three-dimensional display. A model of this kind can be misleading unless it is borne in mind that the actual stand will be viewed at ordinary eye level. Despite this handicap, models give a much more accurate idea of the final result than do artist's impressions—which can be most misleading.

Construction of the Stand

Where time permits, it is usual to submit the plans and specifications to two or three contracting firms for tendering. The designer can suggest suitable firms; but there is a wide choice, and some of the smaller firms may be much cheaper—although often at the expense of quality and service.

If the exhibition is overseas, consideration will have to be given to whether part or all of the stand should be built on site, or whether the major part of the stand should be constructed in the home country and shipped out for erection on site. The nature of the overseas country in question, the availability of local labour, the type of stand, and the relative costs for transport, will be some of the factors that will influence the decision on this point.

When the tenders have been received, it is wise to make a decision quickly in order that the selected contractor can make an early start on any sections of the stand that are to be prefabricated. This is particularly essential in the case of overseas exhibitions, where transport may take a very long time. Furthermore, exhibitors who have found their stands only half ready at overseas exhibitions owing to shipping strikes or port delays are likely to insist in future that the schedule should be advanced to allow for such unexpected emergencies. All may benefit from this salutary experience!

The designer's responsibilities do not end when the contract has been awarded to a contractor. It is his duty to supervise the construction and erection at all stages, and to commission the lettering, photographs, etc; to order the furniture (usually on hire); and to look after the thousand and one details inseparable from the arranging of an exhibition stand. In particular, the designer will study the rules and conditions of the exhibition in question, paying special attention to such points as permissible heights and weights, colour schemes for fascias, rules regarding moving exhibits, live demonstrations, etc. If necessary, the designer will try to negotiate divergencies from these regulations where they are desirable for the success of the stand.

Organisations which exhibit frequently will probably have an exhibition department as a subsection of the public relations department. Where this does not apply, it is essential that one person should be given the responsibility for organising and progressing the many details involved in exhibiting. One of the main duties will be keeping in close touch with the designer and the contractor. However capable and experienced the designer, it is wise for the representative of the client to take a careful and close interest throughout and not to be afraid of expressing an opinion.

The designer, or his assistant, will be on site during the erection and will ensure that the stand is completed in accordance with the specification—and in time for the opening! Keeping to the schedule can be extremely difficult, however, if there are any union troubles at the exhibition. Finally, after the exhibition is over the designer will check all the contractors' accounts, agree or disallow any extras, and certify the final accounts for payment. The savings from this alone may more than cover the designer's fees.

Mention has been made of exhibition rules and conditions. It is rare nowadays to find any objectionable clauses in these rules, but it is always wise to study them closely as they constitute the conditions of the contract between the exhibition organisers and the exhibitors. One point which has given rise to trouble in the past is the attempt by some organisers to retain moneys paid when the exhibition has had to be cancelled. It is now customary for a refund to be paid under such conditions, less a percentage to cover the promoters' reasonable costs.

Drawing up a Timetable

There are so many details to be attended to at various stages in the preparation for an exhibition that it is desirable to draw up a detailed timetable listing all the items that have to be attended to and giving the final dates in each case. The schedule will include such items as: insurance, transport, briefing of staff, telephones, stand cleaning, photography of stand, preparation of literature, entries in the exhibition catalogue, any advertising or other publicity, arranging Press conferences, fire precautions, security and possibly travel and accommodation for staff.

The time between deciding to exhibit and the actual opening day will vary considerably, but for a medium-sized stand about three to four months would be ample. If an exhibition is overseas, or there are other complex factors involved, the preliminary planning may commence as much as a year before the opening date.

Insurance

The need to insure the stand is obvious, but it is also desirable to take out third-party insurance to cover any possible claims by members of the public who may trip over or injure themselves in any way when visiting the stand. Similarly, it is wise to take out comprehensive insurance to cover the staff who will be manning the stand, and their personal effects.

Transport

Transport is fairly simple in the case of home exhibitions, but it becomes a most important aspect of exhibiting overseas. Even when an organisation has its own shipping department, it is advisable to hand over the whole of the transport arrangements to one of the firms which specialise in providing transport and shipping for exhibitions. Otherwise there is a great deal of documentation to deal with, and possibly many complications with the customs on the other side. A specialist firm has experience of meeting the peculiar problems that arise, and has methods of cutting red tape and short-circuiting complicated procedures.

Staff Travel and Accommodation

It is usual to hand over the arrangements to a firm of travel agents with experience in the part of the world concerned. If a considerable number of staff is involved, however, it is sometimes preferable to rent a flat or house and to install domestic staff to run it. At overseas exhibitions it is extremely difficult to get hotel accommodation in the city, and exhibitors often rent hotel accommodation in a nearby town. This is usually preferred to the alternative of lodging in private houses—which is quite expensive, but not very convenient. In all instances, the earlier the arrangements are made the more likely it is to be possible to get what one wants. A reconnaissance on the spot is often the only satisfactory way of securing satisfactory accommodation.

Literature

The type of exhibition will determine the advisability of preparing special literature for distribution, and whether it should be given out freely or only to selected visitors to the stand. Often a thin leaflet is prepared for wide distribution, and a more detailed booklet for restricted issue. If the exhibition is overseas, it is essential that the printed material should bear the name of the country of origin, and it may be necessary to pay duty in some countries even when it can be proved that it is to be distributed free of charge. The question of language may also arise; the utmost care should be taken to ensure the accuracy of any foreign language texts used.

The Exhibition Catalogue

It is usual for exhibitors to be offered a free entry in the exhibition catalogue, but the copy is often required several months ahead. In addition, it is often possible to have further entries on payment or to take displayed advertisements in the catalogue. This question should receive proper attention, as entries in the appropriate sections of the catalogue are very helpful.

Advertising and Publicity

It may be considered advisable to advertise the company's participation in an exhibition in the trade press, the national press, by posters, or by direct mail. Details of the stand should be sent, of course, to appropriate sections of the press in the hope of securing editorial mention.

Press Conferences

Exhibition organisers usually invite the press to attend on the first morning, or on the previous day, and it is essential to be ready to receive the press on the stand on such occasions. In addition, it may be considered desirable to hold an individual press conference at an earlier date to give information about the stand. This is worthwhile only when the stand is a very special one or there are circumstances which warrant it. A stand prepared for an important overseas exhibition is sometimes set up in the home country for the benefit of the press.

At most exhibitions there is a press office where exhibitors can place press releases and other publicity material for visiting journalists to collect. Care should be taken to replace stocks each day that the exhibition is open, as the exhibition press staff cannot be expected to do this.

Cleaning, Telephones, Security
It is necessary to ensure that arrangements have been made for stand cleaning (and for night sheets if necessary); for hiring furniture, not forgetting ashtrays and waste-paper baskets; that fire requirements have been complied with; and that there are adequate security precautions. Telephones should be ordered, and arrangements made with a florist for flowers and indoor plants if desired.

Staffing and Administration of the Stand
The expenditure on an exhibition stand will be wasted unless adequate arrangements are made for providing suitable staff to man the stand, and attention is given to the management of the stand during the show.

It is not possible to stipulate any optimum size for the staff, since it will depend on so many variables. In most cases it is desirable to have a few general staff plus sufficient technically or otherwise qualified personnel to deal with difficult questions. At overseas fairs it is always necessary to have multilingual staff, and this is very useful at home exhibitions where overseas visitors are likely to come in number. In planning the staff requirements it is necessary to allow for mealtimes, etc, and if the hours are very long it may be necessary to allow for twice the staff that are required to be on duty at any one time.

It is possible to hire exhibition staff from agencies that specialise in this field, but it is a good plan to build up one's own staff register of people who have proved absolutely reliable. As far as possible, it is wise to use staff from within the organisation, since they are likely to be familiar with the background and also have a stake in the success of the exhibit. Irresponsible or negligent behaviour at the stand may jeopardise their future in the organisation, so they are likely to be more trustworthy than staff taken on for the duration of the exhibition.

Control of the stand must be vested in one person, with a reliable deputy. This person in control may be the same individual who has acted as the organiser of the exhibition, and this has the advantage that he or she will be familiar with every detail. This may not be possible if the organisation has stands at other exhibitions at the same time, and then it may be wise to choose the most reliable member of the stand staff. It is essential that this stand manager should be briefed in every detail and should be competent to control the behaviour of the other stand staff. One of his or her jobs will be to prepare a staff roster and to see that punctuality is observed. Another obvious duty is to inspect the stand frequently for cleanliness and orderliness, and to take immediate action to remedy any damage or interference with the lighting or working models.

The need for adequate staff has been emphasised, but it is equally important that they should behave well. Too often a visitor to a stand finds it difficult to attract the attention of the stand attendants who are standing in a corner engaged in earnest conversation. It is often useful to have a private office on the stand for talking with important visitors, but such an office is not intended for the staff to hide in. Teacups spread all over the stand, staff lolling about with cigarettes hanging from their lips, staff chattering together or giggling or all going off to lunch together, are some of the mistakes that a competent stand manager will avoid. Incidentally, if female staff are employed on the stand they should be chosen for their looks and personality as well as for their intelligence or linguistic ability. At overseas exhibitions the interpreters may be locally engaged; and when the stand is of a technical nature, it may be possible to engage the help of local students—provided there is adequate supervision.

Dealing With Inquiries

Everything possible should be done to encourage visitors to ask questions. Some stands are designed in such a way that the visitor has to make a positive effort to enter the stand—having to step up on to a high platform, or having to search for the right part of the stand to enter. Any difficulty of this kind may reduce the likelihood of inquiries. When inquiries are made, they should be answered as fully as possible and details recorded so that in suitable cases the inquiry can be followed up from headquarters. A visitors' book for VIPs is also a desirable adjunct to a stand: people are usually flattered at being asked to sign the book, and it provides a useful reference for follow-up activities.

Some Points to Watch

1   In many exhibition halls the general lighting is poor and it is therefore desirable to make sure that the stand illumination is adequate. Many fine stand designs are spoilt by lack of light.

2   It is generally accepted that an exhibition stand must tell its story three-dimensionally, and that text should be kept to a minimum. Unfortunately, some designers go further and always keep the size of the type to a minimum! Apart from the fact that visitors are unlikely to bother to read very small type, there may be many whose vision is inadequate.

3   Some stands are designed without any thought of storage space or room for hats and coats. It is always possible to make some suitable provision for this at the design stage, but not so easy when the stand has been completed.

4   Even when a stand is in a shell scheme it can be made to stand out by good design. Illumination and the wise use of colour can prevent that box-like appearance that is often a weakness of shell schemes.

5   A good stand is wasted if it is not visited. It is necessary, therefore, to devote considerable thought to methods of securing the attendance of those likely to be interested. The promoters of the exhibition will publicise it in general terms, and this should be backed up by sending invitations to suitable people—not forgetting universities and technical colleges, women's organisations, and similar sources of desirable visitors.

6   If a stand is on the ground floor and is visible from the balcony, care should be taken to see that the appearance of the top of the stand is not untidy, as this can make a very bad impression.

7   It is usually necessary to obtain permission from the organisers for any flashing signs, noisy machinery, and any other exhibits that may interfere with the comfort of nearby exhibitors. It is also always wise to contact, at an early stage, the exhibitors who have the adjacent stands in order to ensure that there is no undue clash in style or colour.

8   Photographs of the stand are useful for publicity and record purposes. It is usually rather difficult to get really good photographs of an exhibition stand, and it is therefore wise to use a specialist

photographer in preference to a press or agency one. Photographs of stands are often taken at night, as it may be impracticable to photograph the completed stand before the exhibition opens and it is likely to be difficult for the photographer to work properly while the exhibition is open. In addition to photographs of the stand, it is desirable to make arrangements for news pictures to be taken when VIPs visit the stand.

9 Pilfering is always a problem at public exhibitions, but the most dangerous time is after the exhibition finishes and before dismantling actually commences. There have been cases when a large and valuable carpet has been stolen even though the actual stand was on top of it!

10 It is essential to do nothing at an exhibition which may conflict with union regulations, as any infringement may cause a strike of the whole labour force in the exhibition.

11 If it is intended to dispense hospitality on the stand, it is necessary to see that proper facilities for this are included in the design. It is desirable that the bar and entertaining area should be screened from public view. In some exhibitions the dispensing of alcoholic beverages on stands is not allowed.

12 The electrical wiring plan for the stand should cover all likely needs, not forgetting a point for the vacuum cleaner if the stand is carpeted. Often a fan for cooling or heating is essential, as temperatures may run to extremes.

Exhibiting Collectively
There are many advantages if companies can exhibit collectively overseas. It can increase the impact, and therefore improve results, while at the same time reducing the cost to all participating. Such collective exhibiting is organised in the UK by the Department of Trade and Industry in conjunction with a chamber of commerce or a trade association. Many other countries run rather similar schemes to help companies exhibit collectively.

Since 1957, the British Government has made a very substantial financial contribution designed to encourage collective British participation at approved overseas trade fairs and exhibitions. This financial help was stepped up considerably about 1965, and has proved one of the most successful parts of the Government's export promotion activities. The amount of financial assistance has been scaled down recently.

This government assistance has led to British industry making increased use of joint ventures at trade fairs throughout the world. The author organised over 250 joint ventures of this kind within a seven-year period, and the venues ranged the five continents of the world.

The British Government also organises British pavilions at certain exhibitions where national pavilions are customary. Financial assistance to British companies participating in these pavilions is also substantial, but is worked out on a different basis from joint ventures.

It is often difficult to assess the value of participation in a particular exhibition or trade fair, but many exhibitors sell the equipment they display and this covers their costs—apart from other longer term results. In a number of countries special quotas or allocations of foreign currency are made available for trade fairs, and this fact can make participation worthwhile for many companies.

An interesting way of assessing the value of participation in a trade fair is to equate the number of serious visitors to a stand with the cost of sending a salesman to visit *them*.

Organising a Complete Exhibition

Most of this chapter has been devoted to considering the methods by which an organisation takes a stand in an established exhibition at home or overseas. Sometimes the public relations department will be called upon to organise a complete exhibition, and this brings added responsibilities. The problem is mainly one of organisation, for it is possible to engage the services of an architect-designer to advise on the layout and design of an exhibition and to act as the coordinating designer. The additional problems will include crowd control, reception of distinguished visitors, liaison with the police, providing a press office, attending to advance publicity, and keeping all exhibitors or divisions of your organisation informed of the arrangements.

The desirability—or otherwise—of a formal opening needs careful consideration. It is probably not necessary unless a really newsworthy personality can be secured to open the event. If an opening ceremony is held, check carefully on audibility of speeches and freedom from extraneous noise.

Other special exhibiting problems arise if the organisation is exhibiting at an agricultural show, or at some other exhibition which takes place in the open air. In such cases it would be necessary to build a pavilion, possibly tented, unless mobile vehicles are used as a basis for the exhibit.

To go to the other extreme, an exhibition may take place in a public library. Here all that would be required might be some well-designed screens on which to display photographs, text and other descriptive matter. Specially designed screens for use in this way are obtainable, and the cost is comparatively low. The smaller the exhibition, the more need there is for clean, decisive design which will make the most of available space but will not confuse the visitor by confronting him with a confused jumble of information.

Many provincial towns are poorly supplied with exhibition halls, but some of the larger department stores are able to provide facilities for exhibitions to be held on their premises. Alternatively, it may be possible to secure suitable accommodation in a hotel. Many new hotels incorporate special exhibition and conference suites.

Feedback from Exhibitions
Many companies ignore the benefits that can accrue from bringing back from exhibitions photographs, video-tape or press reports that could be used in the company's house journal or general publicity. Exhibitions should be regarded as part of a company's regular activities, not as isolated events.

Exhibitions combined with Conferences
It is quite usual nowadays for exhibitions to be supported by conferences and *vice versa*. This is both from financial considerations and because these two types of event are mutually supportive.

7 Film and audio-visuals in public relations

Film is a powerful medium of public relations, and its use dates back to the increasing popularity of the documentary film in the 1930s. The function of documentaries has been taken over by television, but there is still a very important place for film in public relations as a medium of communication, instruction, marketing, research, etc.

The increasing popularity of video recorders, and the widespread availability of film on video has given a new impetus to this medium of communication.

Videos are frequently made for free distribution for information, promotion or sales objectives. Some house journals have been replaced by 'house' videos.

Britain can rightly claim to be the cradle of documentary films. Many extremely good ones are still being made in the United Kingdom and elsewhere, but unfortunately many poor films are also being made, and in some instances it is difficult to understand how such exciting subjects can be made so dull. Common faults of industrial films are that they are too long or attempt to cram too much detail into one film.

When to make Films
It is not necessary for public relations personnel to be trained film makers, but it is necessary to have an adequate appreciation of film technique in order to be able to advise on the use of film in an organisation and to act as liaison with the film production company

when a film is being made. It is sometimes necessary to support the producer against unreasonable demands for the inclusion of items that do not fit into the pattern of the film.

Films play an important part in teaching, education, training and research, but it is their use in public relations that we are concerned with here.

Before embarking on film making it is essential to consider three fundamental points:

1 What is the object of the film?

2 For what audience is the film intended and can this audience be reached successfully?

3 How much money can be spent on the film and its distribution, and could this money be spent to better advantage in other ways?

It is on these basic questions that public relations practitioners should be competent to advise.

A film should be conceived in a very precise way. It must be aimed at a specific audience, with the intention of imparting information or putting over a particular point of view. Film has the power, shared only by television, of bringing audiences into direct communication with facts and ideas through the senses—sight and hearing—and the emotions. It is only worth making a film if the intended audience can be defined and if there is a reasonable prospect of being able to reach it. A small influential audience may sometimes justify the total expense of the film, but it is a true anomaly that films made specifically for a particular audience often have a surprising success with a much wider public. This possibility does not excuse the need to define audiences in advance.

The only way to acquire a critical appreciation of industrial films is to see as many different ones as possible. Industrial film festivals are held periodically in many countries, and provide an excellent opportunity of viewing a wide variety of public relations films and of comparing their production, direction and presentation.

Assessing the Audience
The audience to be reached is either the general public through the commercial cinema or television (the 'theatrical audience'), or other

audiences which are classified as 'non-theatrical audiences'. These audiences may be home and/or overseas. These two groups of audiences will react better to different methods of approach, and often require different techniques in film production. It is comparatively rare that a film will prove equally successful for these two types of audience, but it is sometimes feasible to make two different versions of the same film.

Theatrical Audiences

Television audiences can be reached in two ways: either by advertising films where the showing time is bought from the commercial television company, or by feature films of general interest which may be acceptable to both the BBC and to the commercial television contractors. The television companies are usually prepared to show good quality documentary films, but they insist that there be no direct advertising and that any reference to the sponsor be indirect and incidental.

Cinema audiences are reached in much the same way: either by advertising films or by general interest films which are shown for their entertainment value. Such films must be of high quality and artistic standard, and because the film must avoid advertising it is more likely to be made by an industry than an individual company. In fact it is seldom worthwhile for a company to make a film for theatrical distribution alone, since the message must be so indirect. An exception to this general rule is when the product is of national interest such as motor cars, steel, oil, gas or electricity; or when the film is made for showing in a town which is dominated by the firm's own employees.

The making of an industrial film for cinema distribution is always something of a gamble, and the possibilities should be discussed with the producer at an early stage. It is desirable to endeavour to get a film renter to agree that the script is acceptable to him before production commences, but it is unusual for a renter to agree to distribute a short film theatrically until he has seen the finished film. If cinema distribution is considered to be very important, it is wise to engage the services of a film company with a good record of achieving such distribution for its films.

Films may achieve either TV showing or cinema distribution—very seldom both in the case of documentary films.

Non-theatrical Audiences

Most public relations films are made with non-theatrical audiences in mind. Such audiences can be grouped into two main categories.

Existing Audiences. These consist of societies and associations which have been formed for social or professional reasons. This includes clubs, schools, women's guilds, youth centres and many other organisations. Many of these will have their own projection equipment. The distribution of films to these self-equipped groups is a relatively easy matter, and the usual way of reaching them is through the film libraries.

Many existing audiences have no projection facilities of their own, but are anxious to see films which interest them. In such cases it is necessary to provide both equipment and an operator, and the sponsor may even have to hire a suitable hall or cinema. It is possible to hire a mobile projection unit, and many cinemas are available for hire during the mornings.

Invited Audiences. These may consist of half a dozen company directors, members of the press, or several hundred of the general public. Films are sometimes shown to shareholders to give them an idea of the company's activities.

Making the Film

In making a film it is wise to use the services of an established film company unless specialist knowledge is available within one's own organisation. It is possible to make good films oneself, using freelance producers and cameramen, and it works out much cheaper; but this is a course to be adopted with caution. In general, one gets the film one pays for, and too parsimonious a film budget will be reflected in the result.

The established film companies charge considerably more than some private producers, but the sponsor can usually expect a much higher standard of production if he deals with a well-established company, fully equipped and employing a regular staff of high-grade technicians.

It is important to choose a producer with whom the sponsor will be able to work harmoniously and who inspires confidence.

The most valuable guide to the ability of a producer is to see some of his recent films. A producer should be pleased to arrange such a show, and it will permit an assessment of the technical standard of the films and give an idea of the producer's method of tackling different subjects. The producer should also be willing to give some idea of the cost of the films shown. This will provide an approximate idea of the likely cost of the film in prospect.

The Sequence of Operations

Once a producer has been chosen, it is necessary to furnish him with a statement of the policy on the film, which is known as a brief. The brief will normally include information on the following:

1   *The Object of the Film.* This should state clearly what it is hoped to achieve by the use of the film. This statement will be the producer's main guide throughout his subsequent work on the film.

2   *Audience.* It is important that the producer should be given a clear indication of the types of audience for which the film is intended.

3   *Content.* This should list all the material which it is hoped can be included in the film. The relative importance of the items should be given to the producer and editor as a guide to the intended emphasis of the film.

4   *Length.* This must be stated, but it will be influenced by the cost of the film and its possible use on television.

5   *Facilities.* Details should be given of the facilities that will be available during the production of the film. These may include library information, use of factory staff or technicians, etc.

6   *Time Factor.* It is desirable to state the date when the finished film is required.

7   *Distribution.* The producer needs to know the methods of distribution by which it is planned to reach the principal audience.

8   *Cost.* It is necessary to give the producer a clear idea of the budget.

9   *Contacts.* The contact between producer and sponsor will normally be through the public relations staff. It may be desirable in certain cases, however, to appoint a special liaison officer who will be able to ensure that the producer and film director will receive full cooperation and all the facilities they may need.

The producer will study this complete brief and will, in due course, present proposals for making the film. There should be very full discussion at this point, as this is the best time to make sure that the producer has the right idea of what the sponsor wants to achieve from the film.

The next stage is the investigation. This is the period of study by the producer and the writer in which they assimilate the necessary knowledge and background to plan the film. They visit any factories or installations to be filmed and meet the people involved, working in close cooperation with the liaison officer (and the technical adviser, where the theme of the film merits it).

From the investigation, the writer prepares the treatment. This is the written presentation of the film, presented in such a way as to give a clear picture of the proposed shape and contents. The presentation of the treatment is the first approval stage, and all members of the sponsor's organisation who will have to approve the film should study the treatment, criticising it on its general approach, content, and method of presentation.

The producer should now be able to give a fairly accurate indication of the cost of making the proposed film, and the sponsor has thus the first real indication of the ultimate cost. At this stage it is possible to cancel the film by paying a previously agreed fee for the investigation and treatment.

Assuming that it has been agreed to proceed on the basis of the submitted treatment, the next step is the preparation of the shooting script. A number of technical questions have to be discussed including animation, music and use of commentary or dialogue.

The shooting script is the blueprint of the film. It is usually laid out in two columns. On one side the visuals are set out shot by shot, and in the other column the appropriate sounds (words, music, effects, etc) are set out opposite the visual shots to which they apply. This is a very detailed document and will form the basis for the contract which will cover the making of the film. It is essential that this shooting script should be scrutinised very closely and any queries discussed with the producer.

When the shooting script is received, it should be accompanied by a firm quotation for the production of the film with details of how the prices are arrived at. This quotation will be covered by contract, and provided there are no major alterations at a later date this should be the final cost of the film. When the contract is signed, the costs of investigation, treatment and script writing are normally included within the total price of the film.

Shooting the Film

If there is no extended travelling involved, the actual shooting of a typical public relations film may take between three weeks and two months. In order to work efficiently, pre-planning is necessary—as the camera team will not shoot the film in the order of the shooting script, but in the most convenient and economic manner. For example, all the shots in a particular location will be taken on one visit if possible. On outdoor locations the weather may be a great hindrance to the maintenance of the programme.

It is advisable to ask that a number of still pictures should be taken during shooting, as these often prove very useful later on for publicity purposes. Enlarged prints from the actual film are seldom entirely satisfactory.

The Rough Cut

When the shooting has been completed, the editor arranges the various shots in their correct sequence and produces the rough cut. This is the first version of the film, and visually it is fairly rough. The visual tricks—called opticals—which are used to transport the viewer from one scene to the next, are not inserted. The commentary has not been recorded, and the rough cut is thus projected silent but the commentary may be read over the mute film.

This is the most important approval stage. The sponsor can suggest the deletion of scenes, or the alteration of the length of shots where it is considered advisable in order to influence the emphasis of the film. Any basic alterations or new scenes demanded at this stage will probably be the cause of extra cost, but this should not be shirked if any rethinking is essential. Assuming the rough cut has been agreed, the length of the commentary or dialogue can be considered, and the screening time of the visuals increased if necessary to accommodate the commentary. It is a poor film, however, that relies too heavily on the commentary.

The Fine Cut

When the rough cut has been approved, the editor and other technical staff proceed to the preparation of the fine cut. Opticals are added, and the film can be shown in its final form for approval. The music, sound effects and commentary are now recorded, and the picture and sound tracks are married. The show prints can be made and the film is complete.

Counting the Cost

Film making should not be entered into lightly, for it is bound to be a costly operation. It is, however, a very effective medium of public relations when the subject lends itself to film treatment and distribution can be organised successfully.

There are no fixed prices in the film industry, and it is thus difficult to form any accurate idea of costs before the treatment has been prepared by the writer. This is because in the cost of making films the labour component varies from about fifty per cent of the total in live action films, to about eighty per cent of the total cost in cartoons or animated films.

Film producers who have a long series of successful films to their credit will naturally charge more than up-and-coming ones, but whoever makes the film there are always certain fixed factors which govern the overall cost.

Colour or Black and White

Public relations films should be made in colour for best results, but there are a few exceptions to this general rule. For example, if the film deals mainly with machinery, colour may be unimportant compared with the function of the machines, and in some cases to use colour may be to reduce the dramatic effect. Another instance is when it is necessary to include library material which is only obtainable in black and white. Each case should be considered on its merits, and due regard should be given to the advice of the producer.

Sound

Few films can be made without the use of synchronous sound, but it does of course add considerably to the cost of production. If the sound is to be shot on location, a sound-recording crew and equipment have to be taken to the site; and if it is shot in studios, this involves the usual studio costs. It is often difficult to get amateurs to speak convincingly even when they are talking about their own jobs, and it is often necessary to use trained actors.

In making public relations films recorded music is generally used. If the film relies on its musical accompaniment to a marked degree, however, it is well worth considering the commissioning of a specially composed musical score.

If the film is to include a commentary, this is recorded when the film has been completed and is dubbed on to the sound track. If a film is intended for distribution in non-English speaking countries, this should be made known to the producer from the outset. Foreign language prints will have to be made, and the film will be made with two sound tracks—one carrying music and effects, and the other the commentary.

The importance of careful pre-planning is emphasised by the fact that, when sound and picture are finally married, sound is printed many frames ahead of the appropriate picture; if an alteration in the film is demanded at a late stage, the taking out of a length of film and the insertion of a new shot thus becomes a difficult and costly business.

Animation

Certain types of films are more effective if they are made partly or wholly in the medium of cartoons or puppets, but this process is very expensive. In technical films, diagrammatic work may be better than straight visuals and much cheaper than cartoon. For animation there is thus a choice between cartoon, puppets or diagrammatic treatment. These techniques might add very considerably to the cost of the film.

It is very desirable for the sponsor to decide in advance how many copies will be needed, as otherwise considerable delays are likely. It is always advisable to have extra copies in order to be able to achieve the widest possible exposure.

Distributing Films

The distribution of the film to theatrical and non-theatrical audiences must be tackled in different ways.

The most profitable way of showing films to non-theatrical audiences is to arrange special showings for an invited audience. In this way it is possible to control the choice of those who are to see the film, and it may be supported by a speech about the film or about the organisation which made it. Suitable hospitality can also be arranged prior to the film or after it.

Overseas Distribution
Public relations films are often suitable for wide distribution overseas. This can be achieved by the sponsor's own overseas representatives or agents; by selling copies to overseas film libraries; or with government help.

Using Films at Exhibitions
Films can reach a specialised audience at exhibitions. Exhibitors can show their films on a section of their stand, or in some cases can hire a suitable room elsewhere on the exhibition premises.

When exhibitors show films on their own stand, it may be in order to have an eye-catching focus of interest or to tell a story that is not easy to portray by ordinary exhibition display techniques. A number of visitors to the stand can be addressed more efficiently and expeditiously by a film than could be done individually by the stand staff. It is also possible to offer the commentary in a number of different languages to the audience by using earphones. This technique has been used very effectively at a number of overseas exhibitions using four 35-mm cinema projectors coupled together. One projector shows the film with the sound track in English; the other three do not project a picture but merely have a sound track in the chosen language.

There is a choice of two methods of showing films on exhibition stands: either by the provision of a small auditorium area on the stand—preferably with suitable seating—or by the use of an endless film loop projected automatically and continuously from a special self-contained unit. Both these methods use 'back projection'. The picture is thrown on the back of a translucent screen and viewed from the front, thus leaving the viewing area unencumbered by the projection equipment. Naturally only small audiences can be reached by these methods, and the sound level must be kept low enough to avoid interference with normal conversation on other parts of the stand or on neighbouring stands.

If films are to be shown elsewhere in the exhibition, it is advisable to check that the equipment is satisfactory. It is desirable to have fixed times of showing and to publicise these adequately on the stand. A ticket system may also be desirable in order to avoid over-crowding and possible disappointment to visitors. The acoustics of the room may mar the shows. Some of the 'spare' rooms at exhibition halls are completely bare, and are so resonant that recorded speech becomes difficult to follow.

At some exhibitions the organisers arrange film shows as one of the attractions for visitors. The programme is made up by the organisers from films available, and exhibitors are able to offer films for inclusion.

Audio-Visual Communication

Film strips provide a half-way house between colour slides and the fully animated cinema film. Film strips are much cheaper to produce than films, but are able to provide greater continuity and cohesion than slides and can thus be extremely useful in certain clearly defined fields.

Film strips usually consist of a series of still pictures photographed on a strip of 35-mm film. They can be used merely as a series of pictures projected in predetermined order to illustrate a live lecture, or they can be used in conjunction with recorded sound. The former method is seldom used now except for elementary teaching in schools, but the latter method is being used increasingly in the USA and in the United Kingdom.

The advantages of using recorded sound as opposed to a live lecturer are two-fold. First, the method of telling the story can be standardised in the most effective form. Second, the whole range of recorded sound (eg music, dialogue, effects, etc) can be used to dramatise the story.

The pictures are usually in colour and can be actual photographs, cartoons, diagrams or drawings. The pictures are changed at the predetermined points to correspond with the recorded sound, either manually in response to an audible signal or automatically by means of an inaudible signal recorded on the sound track.

Film strips with automatic sound accompaniment are often known as 'talkiestrips', and they are the cheapest of the recognised methods of simultaneous visual and aural communication. They require skilful writing and direction if they are to be effective.

Multiscreen Presentations

A very good dramatic effect can be achieved by the use of multiple slides and carousels combining to give a picture on a large screen. The sophisticated effect which results has been used successfully at exhibitions and for special demonstrations.

Overhead Projectors

A very convenient method of illustrating a talk or a lecture is by using an overhead projector. This is a fairly simple instrument which, by means of a mirror, projects a transparency on to a screen. An advantage is that the lecturer faces the audience and has the projector close to hand. Film or any other kind of transparency can be used to project illustrations, tables or lists and part of the copy can be covered and uncovered as required.

Closed Circuit Television (CCTV)

CCTV has many uses. It can be used to enable a large audience to follow closely intricate demonstrations or to transmit the proceedings of a lecture or meeting to overflow meetings, nearby or at a considerable distance.

8 The Use of the Spoken Word

The spoken word is the oldest means of communication between people, and it still remains a very powerful medium of public relations—despite the competition of the printed word. It is only necessary to recall the speeches of Churchill, Kennedy, and Hitler to realise the possibilities for good or evil of a good orator.

Speaking in Public
One of the occupational requirements of public life is to be asked to speak at public meetings, conferences, luncheons, or dinners. The preparation of speeches is often the task of the public relations department. This is common today in both government and corporate public relations. A short speech, delivered with feeling, will always carry more weight than a long address read carefully from a prepared script. Too many speeches are prepared for good readability afterward rather than for their effectiveness as they are being delivered.

If a person lacks confidence in speaking, or if he or she speaks badly, great benefits can come from taking a course at one of the speech-training schools. It is not easy to suggest to a chief executive that he or she should take lessons in public speaking, but the attempt should be made to achieve the desired result by indirect methods. It can be suggested, for example, that since the executive will be required on occasion to speak on television, a rather nerve-racking ordeal, a certain amount of preparation is desirable. It is possible to mention that politicians take instructions on how to be at their best on television, despite their obvious familiarity with public speaking. Another method is to arrange for the speech to be taken down on a tape recorder or on videotape while it is rehearsed. The playback may convince the chief executive that he or she could benefit from some special training. There is no disgrace in needing advice on public speaking any more than there is in needing coaching for tennis or golf.

Contrary to popular belief, it is not necessary to start and end a speech with an anecdote, particularly if that anecdote is quite unrelated to the subject of the speech. A good story is sometimes worth telling, however, provided it is really funny and well told.

There is plenty of sense in the old saying that a good speech should be like a dress: long enough to cover the subject but short enough to be interesting; and in the advice given to the young person about to speak in public for the first time: stand up, speak up, and shut up. Very often an excellent speech is spoiled by being prolonged unnecessarily. Few speakers can hold the attention of their audience once they start to repeat themselves. Some people are good speakers but have irritating mannerisms, such as rocking backward and forward on their heels or blinking excessively. These mannerisms are usually a sign of nervousness, and the speaker is unaware of them; but once he or she knows, they can usually be avoided.

It is possible to help a speaker in a number of ways. For example, microphones should always be tested beforehand and adjusted for height as required. The lectern should be in a convenient position and fitted with a reading light. If a blackboard is to be used, it is essential to have chalk and an eraser handy. These are obvious points, but they are often overlooked. It is also a help if someone is deputed to see that doors do not slam when people enter or leave while a speech is in progress. Lastly, it is encouraging for a speaker if the front rows are filled. Left to themselves, people will often fill side seats and the back rows, making a speaker feel isolated and the task of communicating more difficult.

Microphone Technique

It is strange that so many people have an aversion to speaking into a microphone. Even when one is provided, it is common to see a speaker push it aside and try to manage without it. If he or she has a naturally resonant and powerful voice, well and good; but so often the people who object to using a microphone are the very ones who need its help. A modern microphone, in any case, does not require one to speak *into* it, but merely *toward* it—and in an ordinary voice. Where there is a panel of speakers on a platform who remain seated while speaking, it is useful to have a microphone on the table in front of each speaker. A neck microphone is very useful if a speaker is moving about.

A good speech can have a more lasting effect than any other single medium of public relations. It is therefore worth a considerable amount of effort to ensure that it is the right speech for the right occasion, delivered by the most able orator in his or her best manner and under the most propitious circumstances. This is the counsel of perfection which, if seldom achieved, is nevertheless well worth striving for.

The Voice of the Firm
Telephone technique is often the Achilles' heel in an organisation's relations with the outside world. Even in instances where meticulous attention is paid to every factor affecting the image of the firm, the telephone technique is often forgotten or ignored.

In many instances, the telephone operator or receptionist is the first member of an organisation with whom an outside person makes contact, and the manner of the receptionist may play an important part in the first impression received—proverbially so important. The receptionist needs to sound courteous, alert, interested, and cheerful. He or she should convey courtesy, competence, efficiency, and friendliness. Proper telephone training will do much to establish a positive image for an organisation.

Telephone operators should be given good conditions under which to work, and adequate arrangements should be made for relief by trained personnel during breaks, holidays, or sickness. It is equally important to ensure that there are sufficient incoming telephone lines and an adequate number of internal extensions. The need for good telephone manners applies throughout the organisation, right up to the top.

Getting calls yourself
When telephoning journalists or editors it is important to make the

connection yourself instead of asking your secretary or a colleague to do so. It is impolite to expect a journalist to wait while your secretary tries to find you to connect the call.

It is the duty of public relations to see that the voice of the firm is courteous, but the work of daily supervision of the telephone is more appropriately the duty of the office or staff manager. The public relations director's responsibility is to assure that a telephone procedure exists that provides a courteous, responsive image and that it is being used.

There are occasions when some organisations receive such a rush of telephone inquiries that it is not humanly possible to answer each call immediately. The problem can be solved by using automatic answering equipment.

Speaking Clearly in Prose

It is not only on the public platform that the spoken word has a significance in public relations. In practically every aspect of everyday life the words used can promote or hinder mutual understanding. This is even more important in the words used in documents, regulations and letters.

The British Civil Service had at one time the reputation of being able to make the simplest statement quite unintelligible. The views of Sir Winston Churchill on this point were well known, and may have inspired the Treasury in 1948 to ask Sir Ernest Gowers to write a book on English for use by officials. Everybody in public relations should possess copies of his two books: *Plain Words* and *ABC of Plain Words,* and should take to heart the advice given on the use of good English. In the prologue to the first book, Gowers discusses the fact that very few people can write clearly and concisely in the first draft, and yet time spent on redrafting and polishing a letter or document may be time needed for even more important work. This is indeed a dilemma common to all in public relations. It is worth quoting Gowers on this point: 'There is a happy mean between being content with the first thing that comes into your head and the craving for perfection that makes a Flaubert spend hours or even days on getting a single sentence to his satisfaction. The article you are paid to produce need not be polished but it must be workmanlike.' This quotation might well be printed above the desk of all who prepare press releases. (Sir Edward Gowers' two books have been revised by

Sir Bruce Fraser and are available in one volume as *The Complete Plain Words* (HMSO).)

Pedantry is certainly not desirable, but it would be a good thing if all in public relations did their best, by example and advocacy, to preserve the correct meaning of words and to save the English language, or their own national language, which is such an important medium of public relations, from progressive adulteration.

The Civil Service has no monopoly of the people who have the knack of making the simplest statement extremely obscure and complicated when they express it in a letter or memorandum. It is salutary to examine a sample selection of the letters sent out by any organisation. It is fairly certain that many will be ambiguous and some may be quite misleading. Such sampling of correspondence is carried out in some large organisations, where it has led to a progressive improvement in standards of letter-writing.

Cultivate a preference for using good English instead of jargon or buzz words. The following are a few of the author's pet aversions with the better word in brackets.

1. Anticipate (expect).
2. Ascertain (find out).
3. At this moment in time (now).
4. Experience (have).
5. Gone missing (disappeared).
6. Inasmuch as (since).
7. In lieu of (instead of).
8. Locate (find).
9. Per annum (yearly).
10. Terminate (end).

Follow the KISS rule in both writing and speaking. Keep it short and simple—KISS. This means using short sentences and making statements logically and simply. A good principle in public relations practice!

9 *Advertising and public relations*

Claim was made in Chapter 1 that advertising is logically a part of public relations since it affects relationships between an organisation and the public, and that in future it may become common for the person in charge of public relations to be responsible also for advertising.

It is unnecessary to examine here in detail the practice of advertising, since there are many good textbooks which deal with this subject, but there are a number of aspects of the subject that are of particular concern to those engaged in public relations and which thus merit attention here.

'Prestige' Advertising

Under modern conditions, it is not enough to make a good product, to market it, distribute it, and promote and sell it efficiently. Even a good product may not succeed if the policies of the manufacturer are weak or misunderstood by the public. It is necessary for a company to be a good member of society, and to let it be demonstrated to the public at large that it is playing a useful part in society. This is the reasoning behind the so-called 'prestige' or 'institutional' type of advertising, but it is also borne in mind by those planning any advertising campaign.

Prestige advertising is probably the most difficult of all forms of advertising, which perhaps explains why so often it fails to make the most of its opportunities. There are two main types of prestige advertising. One sets out to tell the public of the massive contribution that the company is making to the nation's welfare. The second type of prestige advertising is less direct in its approach, seeking to educate or inform on matters of public interest and merely including the name of the sponsoring company.

Before embarking on prestige advertising it is essential to define the objectives clearly, and to know what type of reader it is hoped to reach. It is difficult to draw up a satisfactory media list as the usual criterion of cost per thousand readers may have little relevance. In some forms of prestige advertising the desired readership may be very small.

Prestige advertising has an important part to play in support of exports. There are more than fifty major international journals, such as *Reader's Digest* and *Time,* which have a significant circulation across frontiers. The quantity of advertising in these magazines and journals, most of it of a prestige nature, is increasing year by year. This is a sure sign that it is producing results.

Financial Advertising
In financial public relations, advertising can at times be of great importance. If a company wishes to communicate quickly with its shareholders or with the general public the most effective way is by taking display advertising in the national press or on television. This is particularly the case when bids and takeovers are being contested. Rights issues, privatisation and similar circumstances all create a need for large scale advertising.

Editorial Features
There are occasions when the interests of an organisation are adversely affected by certain public misconceptions and it is necessary that the true facts should be presented quickly to the public. Under such circumstances the usual media of public relations would be too slow in their effect, and the answer is to take advertising space to publish the public relations announcement.

Many people believe that newspapers—and, to a lesser degree, periodicals—will not give publicity in their editorial columns to organisations which do not advertise. This is a strongly held belief, but so far as reputable papers are concerned it is without foundation. Editorial staffs work independently of advertising departments, and the criterion for the publishing of a news item or feature is whether or not it is 'news'—not whether it pleases or displeases an advertiser.

In technical and trade journals the same general principle holds good, but there is closer contact between editorial staff and advertisers. When special editorial features are planned, the manufacturers or suppliers concerned are often invited to take advertising in support of the feature: but this should not be a condition of the editorial mention.

In many countries, however, this division between news and advertising is blurred, and it is often necessary to pay for editorial mentions. This practice is to be deprecated but it may be necessary to follow local custom.

Supplements

This leads naturally to the subject of supplements. It has become a common practice for the press to plan special supplements dealing with such diverse subjects as an overseas country, an industry, or the opening of a local supermarket. The purpose of these supplements should be for the interest of readers, but too often it is only to attract additional advertising revenue. This is not true in every case, for often a paper is prompted to plan a supplement by a public relations approach.

In general, supplements succeed better in their public relations aspect than in their advertising value. For this reason there is a growing resistance by advertisers, who resent particularly any 'pressure salesmanship' designed to force them to take advertising contrary to their better judgment. Supplements are even less desirable when the editorial is keyed to the advertising. This type of unbalanced editorial reporting is detrimental to the best interests of the press, and all in public relations should be wary of supporting special press features and supplements except when they are satisfied that there is an honest intention to discuss the subject objectively and impartially. Such comments do not apply to the supplements published by leading national newspapers; these may have a very good public relations effect, although some advertisers question their value as an advertising medium.

Organisation of Advertising

Only in very rare instances will a public relations practitioner need to design or place his own advertising; usually he will work through his advertising department or through an advertising agency. It is desirable, however, that he should cultivate a critical appreciation of advertising practice, become familiar with the methods and practice of advertising, and understand the way in which advertising is organised.

At least ninety per cent of advertising is devoted to the sale of goods and services, and this has led to advertising agencies taking a specialised interest in such problems as marketing, merchandising and market research. The designing and placing of an advertisement for a client is merely the end result of an advisory service calculated to aid the client in a wide range of problems associated with marketing. In very large companies the advertisement director or manager will be competent to deal with much of this himself, using the agency mainly for the design and placing of advertising.

The public relations department or consultant should be competent to advise on the effectiveness or otherwise of particular types of advertising, and should also have views on the type of advertising agency most suitable for different types of campaigns. It is a great pity that this advice is so seldom sought.

SUMMARY
Besides direct consumer advertising (DCA), which constitutes the major portion of the advertising budget, there are many occasions when advertising plays a significant role in a public relations programme. These include publication of the chairman's address at the annual general meeting, announcement of scholarships, competitions or awards, recruitment, product recall, or other requirements for quick and positive communication.

10 The place of research in public relations

Chapter 1 emphasised the need for research before a public relations programme can be planned and of the desirability of measuring results as the campaign gathers momentum.

It is foolish to ignore the advantages of adequate research; it is even more dangerous to rely on it to the exclusion of other ways of reaching decisions. Too much should not be read into the results of a marketing research survey. A margin of error may have to be accepted. The results may indicate trends rather than facts. People may express interest, but they may not finally buy. A research report needs to be read intelligently. The results will depend on what questions were asked, of whom and perhaps when. A problem with research is that respondents may resent being questioned, or be reluctant to give information, or give misleading answers.

In developing countries, where people are less familiar with marketing research, people may fear answering questions because they may suspect some ulterior motive such as the gathering of information for taxation purposes. There may also be taboos and customs which make the collection of information—as in census-taking—very difficult so that false results occur.

Public relations is essentially an art of persuasion, and in order to influence people it is obviously helpful to know as much as possible about the way in which people think and the manner in which they react to particular circumstances. Experience and intuition will provide an answer, but where it is desirable to obtain more factual or statistical data it is necessary to employ the techniques of motivation research, opinion research and market research which have been evolved to provide the answers to problems of this kind.

Increasingly management wants to be certain it is getting value for money and resources devoted to public relations. Research schemes built in to public relations programmes can help to provide quantitative evidence.

The Research Process

Opinion, market, and academic researchers have developed a pattern of research that involves nine basic steps:

1 Statement of the problem.

2 Selection of a manageable portion of the problem.

3 Definition of concepts and terms.

4 Literature search.

5 Development of a hypothesis.

6 Determination of a study design.

7 Gathering of the data.

8 Analysis of the data.

9 Recording of the implications, generalisations, conclusions.

Definitions

Government research is called *social research;* that into market conditions is known as *market research;* while all the forms of research used in advertising, marketing and public relations are more broadly described as *marketing research.*

Professor Michael J Baker *(Marketing: An Introductory Text)* states:

By definition, market research is concerned with measurement and analysis of markets, whereas marketing research is concerned with all those factors which impinge upon the marketing of goods and services, and so includes the study of advertising effectiveness, distributive channels, competitive products and marketing policies and the whole field of consumer behaviour.

There are basically three kinds of research: desk research, ad hoc research and continuous research.

Desk research (sometimes called Secondary Research)

A practical way to fill an information request is through what is known as secondary research. This consists of trying to find out whether data already exists on the subject as a result of surveys or work that others have conducted.

The advantages of secondary research are twofold: (a) it is relatively inexpensive to do. Even if one has to pay a fee for the existing reports, the price is still small in comparison to the cost of conducting the research in the first place, and (b) the information can be obtained relatively quickly. The alternative of conducting new research (interviewing respondents, tabulating results, preparing a report) is usually time consuming.

There may be disadvantages in the use of information from secondary research. The data may not apply exactly to the subject you are interested in. Or, it may not deal directly with the specific group of people (or public) in whom you are interested. For example, you may want to know the views of the population in general, but the survey may have been conducted only among people with a higher level of education; or among lower income groups.

In using secondary research, there is absolutely no control over the manner in which the survey or surveys were conducted. And, the survey data seldom meet the need for the exact information that is being sought. However, when one is looking for an overall indication and/or does not have a budget to conduct research, secondary research may be used and adapted to one's needs. Secondary research can usually provide worthwhile clues to public attitudes.

Ad Hoc Research

This is often called 'Primary or Custom Research'. If desk research does not provide all the required data, it will be necessary to initiate a *single* custom survey or a series of surveys—to supply the information necessary.

Continuous Research

This means a series of surveys—maybe monthly, quarterly, or every 6 months, to record trends. This can be plotted on a graph to show how the situation was changing.

Research involves sample selection, methods of interviewing, questionnaire formulation, tabulation of results and interpretation of results.

Opinion Research
When opinion research is mentioned it includes: national and local opinion surveys and polls, media studies, readership studies, employee or customer attitude surveys and investor relations studies.

Sample Selection
Deciding upon whom to interview in a survey should be determined with one objective in mind: the sample should be representative of the population or of the specific public that is the focus of attention. This point is so basic, but it is often overlooked.

It is not the purpose of a survey to find out what opinions a sample of respondents hold. Rather, the purpose is to gain some insight into how the total population or a specific group as a whole is thinking based on survey results. And this can only be achieved if the sample is as representative of the whole as possible, so that the results may be projected to represent the whole.

It would, for example, be ludicrous if opinions were being sought of the coffee-drinking population on the price of coffee, but the sample was not selected with that goal in mind, and half of the people interviewed in the survey turned out to be non-coffee drinkers.

Probably, the most frequently used sampling procedure is the Quota Sample, which is composed of people who have specific characteristics in common. These characteristics are designated relative to the purpose for which the survey is being conducted. An example of this, as already indicated, is coffee drinkers.

The theory behind quota sampling is that if the sample is made up of a random selection from the group with common characteristics, it will probably be representative of the opinions of the entire group.

The size of the sample depends on the scope of the project. Size is not crucial if the sample is truly representative of the population. Sometimes a strict limit in budget will make it necessary to use a smaller sample. In general, when using the quota sample technique, 200 to 400 interviews among qualified respondents selected randomly will serve as a reasonable minimum sample size.

Methods of Interviewing

Obviously, the best method is the face-to-face contact that is achieved with interviewer and respondent in a personal interview. However, this generally also is the most expensive method, since an interviewer actually has to travel from respondent to respondent to conduct the interviews.

Still, this method has the advantage of greater flexibility. Because of the face-to-face contact, an interviewer can expand the scope of an interview more readily if necessary. This includes the showing of exhibits to the respondent which allows for another dimension. As well, there are subjects where the rapport gained from a personal interview is absolutely necessary to conduct the survey.

Telephone interviewing, which is a less expensive method than personal interviewing, can be more than adequate for many projects and should be considered. There also is an advantage in controlling the project when the telephoning is done from a central location. A supervisor in the room can assure that all interviewers are conducting the interviews in a uniform fashion. In personal interviewing, interviewers are on their own and therefore a pre-interview instruction session is particularly important. And, as already suggested, if the interview is on a sensitive subject or is complicated or lengthy, the telephone interview probably will not be sufficient.

Interviewing by mail eliminates interviewer expenses and is by far the least costly research to conduct. Potentially, it has a great flaw in that those people who send back a completed questionnaire may be different from those who do not respond.

Accordingly, in using a mail survey, there is the risk that the responding sample may not be representative of the whole population or group.

Questionnaire Formulation

One of the fundamental errors made in questionnaire construction is that the original purpose for conducting the research may be overlooked as the questions are drafted. Clearly, one must keep in mind the objective to be achieved and form the questions accordingly.

If a quota sample is used, qualify the respondent as quickly as possible so that time is not wasted with additional questions if the respondent does not qualify. For example: we are conducting a survey about people's reasons why they drink coffee. 'Do you drink coffee?' If the respondent says 'no', terminate the interview; if 'yes', continue.

Design the questions so that the more important ones (to you) are asked after allowing for rapport to develop between interviewer and respondent. The answers by respondents are likely to be more accurate. The initial questions should be useful but not necessarily crucial.

It is always wise to send out a number of questionnaires *before* finalising the text to see if there are any ambiguities.

When there are a number of questions that are related, keep them together in a sequence. This helps the respondent to concentrate. Skipping around distracts the respondent.

If you have a particularly sensitive question, try to save it for the end. In this way, if the respondent baulks at answering and refuses to continue, you will at least have salvaged the remainder of the interview.

Tabulation of Results
While results usually are tabulated in total, question by question, there frequently is much useful information to be gained from tabulation by segments of the respondents. Do men have different opinions than women? Do light coffee drinkers (perhaps two cups a day) think differently than heavy coffee drinkers (perhaps eight or more cups a day)?

Interpretation of Results
Initially, look at the answers to the individual questions. Then determine whether any pattern develops in comparing results to different questions. Cross-tabulation of results may help in your interpretation of them. Heavy coffee drinkers may have different opinions as to the qualities that make for a good tasting coffee than do light coffee drinkers.

In interpreting results, you may find that not all of the questions you had in mind were resolved. It can at times be important to know this as well, that many people are undecided on an issue; or that a sufficient number of respondents are not sure that they will buy a product again.

127

The proper conduct of research necessitates the resolving of a number of factors. However, if research is properly conducted, you will be that much ahead in information at hand and in the facilitation of the decision making process.

Who Should Conduct Research?

If it is to be reliable, and as free from bias as possible, primary research should be conducted by independent experts such as a professional research organisation. Salesmen should never be asked to carry out surveys, neither should other company staff who might bias the enquiry. Very large companies do employ research units (whose services may be commissioned by other firms) but the research staff are skilled specialists. Some of the largest advertising agencies own subsidiary research firms, but they work independently and often for clients other than those of the parent company.

The specialists are psychologists, sociologists and statisticians who understand how to word and design questionnaires, select samples of people, process answers, and interpret results. These are not tasks for amateurs. This also extends to the recruitment, training and supervision of interviewers.

Finding suitable people to conduct interviews can be a problem in developing countries. In the West—and because interviewing is usually an occasional part-time job—interviewers are usually women and mostly either young women of suitable education (eg social science degree) or middle-aged women whose families have grown up. The need is for people with a sympathetic, pleasant, mature but unobtrusive personality. The tendency in developing countries is to employ university students, mainly because they are well-educated and available during vacations. They could be too young and inexperienced sometimes for such work which requires patience and can be very frustrating.

Research in Planning a Public Relations Programme

Any public relations programme must be based on a careful analysis of all relevant facts, and this will often involve a considerable amount of research. For this reason it is unrealistic to expect a public relations programme to be prepared overnight, or for it to yield immediate results. This thought is behind the insistence that public relations should be 'deliberate, planned and sustained'.

Research in public relations is not a separate subject; it is the very essence of successful public relations activity, since it collates the past and present experience of all concerned.

There is an urgent need for research into the results of public relations activity. We know too little about the effects of public attitudes on public action. It is desirable to be able to study the results of past public relations programmes so as to benefit from their success or failure.

11 Conferences, Hospitality*

Organisation of Conferences

Conferences are usually held to discuss policies or to debate matters of mutual interest, but their value lies as much in the opportunity they provide for people to meet and to get to know one another. This advantage is enhanced when wives accompany their husbands, for the family friendships made in this way often last for years.

The organisation of a conference—whether it be a large or small affair—requires careful preparation and detailed execution. Regardless of the purpose of the conference, its arrangement often falls to the lot of the public relations department.

The first requirement for success is to ensure that the venue has audio-visual and other necessary technical facilities. There is no substitute for personal inspection, and a reconnaissance is essential before any final decisions are taken. Not only should the conference hall and the hotels be inspected, but also any places to be visited—including those where meals are to be taken.

If a conference is to have an international attendance, simultaneous interpretation may be necessary. It is unrealistic to expect everybody to understand English!

Many items of printing are required for a conference, and it is an excellent idea to adopt a symbol and a uniform style and colour

---

*The subject of this chapter is dealt with in greater detail in 'Exhibitions and Conferences from A to Z' by Professor Sam Black ISBN 0 903629 02 X published by Modino Press 1989.

scheme. This simple device gives unity to all the arrangements. Apart from the obvious items, it is useful to print luggage labels and car stickers for the use of participants. The same symbol and style should be maintained throughout the arrangements, right up to the printing of the report of the proceedings.

The preliminary notice of the conference sent out to prospective participants should give the fullest possible details of the arrangements, as this will reduce the number of queries which have to be dealt with. However well the preliminary documentation is organised, there are always many formalities to be attended to when participants arrive for registration, and great care should be taken to see that this takes place efficiently and speedily. The main essential is to have sufficient staff knowing what has to be done, and doing it with charm and quiet efficiency. The conference office should be open as late as possible on the night before the conference commences.

There is little doubt that special arrangements will have been made to receive VIPs or other special guests, but it is equally desirable to see that *all* participants receive a cordial welcome. Flowers for the ladies—and cards of welcome in the bedrooms, are two little items that make a deep impression, particularly when some of the delegates have come from afar.

Whatever the nature of the technical or business sessions, skill is needed to plan the programme in such a way that ample time is allowed for meeting together informally between sessions and during free periods.

Every endeavour should be made to keep rigidly to the timetable, and there should be sufficient stewards to shepherd participants quietly, unobtrusively, but firmly. A successful conference needs meticulous attention to detail, but all the organising activity should be quiet and inconspicuous and not too obvious.

It is usual to invite the press to attend the conference, and this question has been considered in Chapter 3. Many conferences incorporate exhibitions or special displays, and it is usually possible to invite local residents to attend at restricted times. A conference, if it is large and well attended, makes a considerable impact on a town, and it is a good plan to let the local people know as much as possible about it, particularly when the subjects under discussion are of general public interest.

Many conferences are supported by exhibitions and *vice versa*. It is essential to make it easy for participants to spend sufficient time at both events.

International conferences of a professional or technical nature have become commonplace, and provide an excellent opportunity for the interchange of ideas and the promotion of international understanding.

Some Thoughts on Hospitality

The art of hospitality in business should be exactly the same as it is in private life. True hospitality does not seek to buy friendship; it is the background to the establishment of cordial and lasting relationships. Critics of public relations insinuate that it consists mainly of wining and dining, and of entertaining lavishly to curry favour or to place other people under an obligation. This type of behaviour does occur at times in the world of business, but it is definitely not a part of professional public relations practice.

The life of a senior public relations practitioner is a busy one, with the telephone ringing constantly and with a multitude of details to be dealt with. It is not easy to settle down to a serious discussion with a visitor in the office, and it is therefore convenient—and pleasant— to fix meetings at lunch time, or over dinner in the evening, when it is possible to eat together and discuss matters quietly and without interruption.

One of the assets of a public relations practitioner is his contacts, and it is necessary to maintain contact with people by meeting them, having a drink together, inviting them to lunch occasionally, and taking the trouble to keep friendships alive.

In addition to having a good knowledge of the media of communication, it is desirable for those in public relations to be knowledgeable about food and drink, the media of entertaining.

Public relations is *not* mainly entertaining, but in the course of a year a public relations practitioner may be called upon to organise a wide variety of social functions and meetings. These may range from a full-scale conference banquet for over five hundred, to a luncheon meeting for eight to twelve journalists, or even a dinner for four.

A luncheon or dinner party should be planned as carefully as any other operation, and all eventualities should be considered and allowed for. The arrangements should be flexible enough to cope with emergencies such as the principal guests arriving late or not arriving owing to last-minute illness, a parliamentary crisis, or other causes.

Even when a function is to be held at a first-class hotel or restaurant, it is essential to leave nothing to chance if the event is to be a complete success. No banqueting manager minds a customer being fussy. Care in selection of the menu and choice of wines usually brings out the best in a *maître d'hôtel,* who is put on his mettle by the interest shown.

There are no firm rules to be followed in the choice of a menu. The important point is to ensure that the food should be appropriate to the occasion, and account should be taken of any known tastes of the chief guests. The menu may also be affected by whether ladies are present or not. Special provision should be made in advance if there are likely to be any guests who may have special religious rules about food. For example, it is wise not to include pork in a menu for a large gathering of possibly mixed religions.

With the increase of vegetarianism it is necessary to ensure that these special dietic needs can be met.

The choice of the menu will naturally influence the type of wine to be served. Whatever the main course, however, it is desirable to offer a choice of white or red wine and if ladies are present they are likely to appreciate a somewhat less dry wine than men. If the occasion is a formal one, it is usual to serve an appropriate wine with each course, but this would be ostentatious at a less formal meal.

There is a great deal of snobbery about wine, but there is a growing appreciation of the finer points and it is wise to flatter the guests by giving them fine wines. It is even more important to see that the wines are served at the correct temperature, but this may be taken for granted at a high-class hotel. At a lesser establishment it is wise to give the matter personal attention.

The prices on the wine list are by no means the best guide to the wines to choose, and it is desirable for all men and women in public relations to acquire a good working knowledge of wine. Since the only way is by trying different types as opportunity permits, this is a part of the apprenticeship in public relations that should appeal to all except the very light-headed.

Use your imagination when planning entertainment, and do not get into a rut. *De luxe* hotels are very similar in most capital cities, and visitors from overseas will probably prefer to visit restaurants with more local colour. In London it is possible to hold events at Livery Halls or other unusual venues.

An easy way of giving a meal an individual character when it is held in a public restaurant or hotel is by having special menus and place cards printed. If they are well designed, they are likely to be kept long after memories of the meal itself have faded.

The remarkable increase in the number of national and international conferences has led to a corresponding increase in the facilities available for meetings and catering in all the major cities of the world. There is thus keen competition to secure conferences and large meetings, and this provides much greater choice than hitherto.

Conference centres and facilities have proliferated worldwide and there is now ample choice for selecting venues for meetings of any size, large or small.

Part 3

Public Relations in Action

12 *Commerce and Industry*

Public relations in commerce and industry is a function of management. It contributes to the successful operation of a company or organisation in proportion to the extent to which it is allowed to play its part. This fact has been accepted by most large companies, but many medium-sized companies have been slow to realise the advantages of organised public relations.

OBJECTIVES OF INDUSTRIAL PUBLIC RELATIONS

There are two main objectives of public relations in an industrial company. The first is to establish contact with three important sections of the public: its customers, its shareholders, and its employees. Securing the mutual understanding and cooperation of these three groups is essential to success. The second objective is to promote the company's services and products in a highly competitive world.

It is necessary to draw a distinction between a public relations attitude and public relations practice. Both are required in industry. The correct attitude toward public opinion should be present from top to bottom in an organisation; the practice should be the responsibility of professionals trained in the art of communication.

Industrial public relations requires a list of priorities in order that available money and manpower are deployed to maximum advantage. It is easy to be tempted into pursuing projects that might yield fruitful results; but there may be more important problems which should be tackled first. The order of priority will not necessarily remain constant, and will require periodic reassessment.

Some very effective public relations is being carried out in industry—both by companies with their own internal public relations departments and by others using consultants—but the general level of attainment is uneven. For example, one company is well organised for press relations and employee relations, but neglects other aspects. Another company devotes all its attention to community relations. The best results come from a properly coordinated plan based on a carefully chosen list of priorities.

An Assessment

The importance of public relations to management decision making in industry was recently emphasised through the observation of the operation and function of a public relations department in a major corporation. The role the public is having on decisions made by top management in industry was readily evident in more than a dozen areas. Technical advancement in the communications field, creating an accessibility to information not available to previous generations, is one of the reasons for an increasing worldwide awareness and interest on the part of the public. An exploding world population straining water, land, forest, and mineral resources, however, is probably the main reason for the public interest in industry decisions.

Management in industry is also finding that it must know much more about the public and the various defined or specialised interest groups within the public which can have an impact on the industry concerned.

Public influence is exerted through the development of government regulation; legal system decisions; lobbying efforts of special interest groups; press coverage, editorial comment, and published letters to the editor; through the withdrawal of product purchasing support; and by public demonstration.

Industry management is rapidly learning that it is less costly to know the probable reaction of its publics to decisions so that courses of action can be planned in advance to educate and promote understanding. It is also learning to avoid decisions causing public reaction that will lead to increased legislation or regulation. Industry is learning that by ignoring or improperly evaluating public reaction, management decisions can be made which in the long range may be detrimental to the welfare of the industry.

Examples of some of the areas in which public opinion and concern are directly affecting management decisions in industry are as follows:

1 Energy conservation.

2 Conservation and preservation of natural resources.

3 Environmental protection. As technological advancements are made and as more is learned about the result of past technological advancement, the public is taking an increased interest in the preservation of the quality of life.

4 Human rights. The advancement in the communications media can be expected to focus public attention on violations of human rights on a worldwide basis.

5 Health, safety, and welfare of employees.

6 Protection of investors. Extensive steps are taken to keep investors and potential investors, through investment analysts, informed about management decisions and the corporation's financial condition.

7 Quality control and safety of products and services. Never before has society been so demanding of consumer protection.

CUSTOMER RELATIONS
Relations with customers depend very much on quality, price, and delivery times, but also very directly on the reputation of the company. Public relations can play a vital part in safeguarding a reputation or in building a new 'public image.' It can also improve methods of communication with existing and potential customers.

FINANCIAL PUBLIC RELATIONS
This specialised sector of public relations has developed rapidly during the last few years. It is perhaps more correctly described as "Investor Relations".

In this field, the public relations consultancy, or in-house department, will usually also be responsible for the financial advertising which can become very important in bid, take-over or rights issue situations. It is essential to be familiar with the increasing number of disclosure regulations and insider restrictions applicable to all deals affecting the Stock Exchange. Different rules may apply to stock exchanges in other countries.

In the past, the sending out of the annual accounts and balance sheets was often the only contact between a company and its shareholders. This annual report, a legal requirement, was often little more than a mass of figures and statistics. It is now common for public relations advice to be sought in the preparation of the report, in order that it may give as much information as possible to shareholders. The design and typography of annual reports have improved beyond all recognition within the past few years.

Annual Reports

It is reported that company annual reports do not rank very high in the list of individual investors' sources of useful information, behind newspapers, stockbrokers and friends. This may well result from the failure of companies in the past to take full advantage of this form of communication.

The final version of an annual report is a product of management consensus, but the public relations adviser usually has the opportunity of designing and presenting the final production.

In the past, some companies' annual reports hid more than they revealed, but the Companies' Acts have made disclosure necessary and it has become recognised policy in many organisations that the printed annual report and accounts should be used as a positive public relations instrument. It is not good policy, however, to publish a lavish annual report if the accounts reveal a loss on the year's working!

Some companies adopt a theme each year for their annual reports, highlighting one aspect of the company's operations at home or overseas. The use of photographs, illustrations, charts and diagrams can make a report attractive enough for each shareholder to want to study and retain; such copies can also be used to attract the attention of potential investors. If the company's operations are very extensive or complicated it may be a good idea to publish a simplified version for the benefit of employees and others interested. This is done successfully by many large companies. The chairman's speech at the annual general meeting is now often published, in full or part, as an advertisement in suitable journals, and this can include an offer to send the full or simplified annual report to those interested.

Companies can make other efforts to keep in touch with their shareholders—for example, by inviting them to film shows, or to open days at factories, sending them copies of house journals or videos, and so forth. The approach will depend on the nature of the company's business.

This branch of public relations can yield good results. The winning of shareholders' sympathy and support can be invaluable in the face of unwanted takeover bids. It can facilitate the raising of further capital by rights issues, and generally strengthen the company's financial standing with the institutions and with banks, suppliers, and others.

The annual general meeting can be made a public relations occasion instead of the mere formality it so often is, and shareholders can be encouraged to attend by holding the meetings in cities where large numbers of shareholders reside. Alternatively, some meetings of the board can be held in locations other than where the company headquarters are located, followed by receptions for shareholders living in the locality. Anything that can bring shareholders into closer touch with the board will serve to strengthen the company and safeguard its existence.

EMPLOYEE RELATIONS

Internal public relations is an extremely wide field. It embraces almost everything—other than pay—which encourages employees to make their maximum contribution to productivity and the prosperity of the company. The field is not sharply defined; it overlaps with personnel, welfare, labour relations and training, and must work in harmony with these other equally important facets of industrial management.

Public relations can contribute to the creation of an atmosphere in which people will work more effectively and willingly and, therefore produce better goods at lower costs; it can initiate suggestion schemes and safety campaigns; it can lessen waste and carelessness and absenteeism; and, perhaps most important of all, it can enable management to communicate more effectively with employees at all levels. The methods used will include house journals (see Chapter 4), joint-consultation techniques, and all the media of communication and information.

In many instances, employees of a company and their families represent a large proportion of the local population, and in such cases careful attention to community relations is particularly essential. Under these circumstances the local press becomes of great importance.

Public relations cannot guarantee to prevent disputes, but a well-conceived public relations programme can play a useful part in eliminating rumours and misunderstanding and lack of information which often lead to industrial action.

An Aid to Recruitment

Very large sums of money are expended on advertising to attract young people and graduates into industry. Public relations could do much more in this connection if it were given the chance, for the reputation of a company is an important factor in recruitment.

Recruits are needed at three levels: school-leavers, graduates, and trained men and women, and obviously a different approach is necessary in each case. Personal contact, direct mail and well-produced publications all have their place but perhaps an even better idea is to try to persuade potential recruits to visit the company's establishments, to meet senior members of the staff, and even to take short initiation courses during vacations. Correct induction procedures are important. This is a very complex problem, affecting many branches of management, but there is no doubt that public relations can make an important contribution to a successful recruiting policy.

Public Relations in Support of Marketing

The main objective of most companies or organisations is to sell their products or services at home and overseas. The role of public relations in improving methods of communicating with existing and potential customers has already been mentioned, but there are many other ways in which public relations assists sales promotion.

Press relations is of prime importance, and this will include the financial press and the technical press in addition to the national and provincial newspapers. The trade and technical press, in particular, form a valuable ally in most forms of sales promotion. It is a remarkable fact that trade press editors experience difficulty in getting news for their editorial columns: news about new methods of production, new raw materials, sales campaigns, and news about personalities or business deals.

There are, in addition, special shopping features in most newspapers and periodicals, and reporters are seeking news of new fabrics, new gadgets, and reliable information on anything that will interest their readers.

It could be argued that product publicity is more akin to sales promotion than it is to public relations. Insofar as it relates to editorial publicity, however, it is usually conducted from the public relations department although it may be a separate sub-section of it.

One development has been the proliferation of special 'weeks' or 'fortnights'. A rather similar idea is the selection of beauty queens such as 'Miss Cotton', or 'Miss British Rail'. These ideas have come from the United States, where every week is devoted to many different types of special pleading. Used with discretion, valuable results can come from the holding of a special week or the crowning of a 'queen', but these are ideas which attract by their novelty and, therefore, should not be used indiscriminately.

Exhibitions, publications, posters, films and advertising all play an important part in industrial public relations, and they have been discussed in earlier chapters.

Liaison with Specialised Groups of the Press

The practice of press relations has been dealt with in detail in Chapter 3, but there is one aspect which has a particular importance in industry although it does also apply in some other fields. The tendency has been for journalists with like interests to band themselves into guilds or associations. Some of the best known in the UK are: the Labour and Industrial Correspondents' Group; the Guild of Agricultural Journalists; the Guild of Motoring Writers; and the Association of British Science Writers; but others are being formed and also a number of groups operate informally.

These groups usually have a secretary who can give useful guidance on suitable dates for proposed facility visits, and in general express an opinion as to whether his colleagues are likely to be interested in information on various subjects. The oldest of these groups is the Lobby in the House of Commons, which is referred to in Chapter 13.

Apart from these formal groups, there are many small groups of journalists or editors who form a natural circle of interest to different sections of industry. For example, the editors of the electrical engineering journals are often invited as a group to informal luncheons or meetings. These meetings are for the purpose of imparting background information and answering questions, and play a very useful liaison function.

The head of a small company will find it beneficial to establish friendly relations with the editor of the local newspaper, who may well be the local correspondent for the Press Association and is thus a link with the outside world. The editor should be invited to look round the factory and to hear about future plans.

Industrial Public Relations Worldwide

Many companies have worldwide interests, and it is desirable to supplement the public relations at headquarters by complementary arrangements in all the areas where the company has significant business interests. This may be achieved by working through the company's foreign agents, by engaging the services of public relations consultants in the countries concerned, or by establishing foreign branch public relations offices.

The foreign agents are usually well informed on local conditions, and may have useful contacts with the local press; but they often represent a number of different manufacturers, possibly from different countries. Even if the agent has the necessary knowledge and experience to promote effective public relations, it is unlikely that he will do it except in a spasmodic manner.

If a company's activities in an area are very substantial, or if there is a subsidiary company operating there, it is probably worth considering the setting up of a locally based public relations office. This provides a closer measure of control than any other method. The alternative is to employ public relations consultants, and this would be the method of choice if the operations in the particular area were not so extensive or perhaps varied in intensity.

Whichever of the two latter methods is adopted, it is desirable that the persons carrying out public relations for the company should be brought to the headquarters in the initial stages and given a thorough briefing on the company and its products and services. The visit would also provide the opportunity for a refresher course on public relations practice as it is understood by the parent company. If personnel in several different parts of the world are concerned, it is a good plan to bring them all to headquarters at the same time for briefing, as this gives them an opportunity of meeting each other and forming a basis for future cooperation. This procedure would cost more than if the head of the public relations department visited the branches, but the beneficial effect of bringing them together for initiation and briefing is worth the additional expense. This can be followed up—say in eight to ten months' time—by visits to the branches.

Working with Others Sharing Common Interests
In public relations there are many opportunities for cooperating with other organisations which are non-competitive but which share common spheres of interest. It is obviously sensible for makers of steel to cooperate with users, for oil companies to work with motor-car manufacturers, for railways to cooperate with large users of freight services, or for airlines to link with makers of aircraft, engines and components. In the field of consumer goods and services there are even more opportunities for cooperation.

When two or more public relations departments are working together on a project, it is most desirable that there be a clear understanding on individual responsibility. For example, if a press conference is held, the arrangements should be the responsibility of one organisation, with the other or others kept fully informed and cooperating to the full in accordance with an agreed plan. Failure to do this results in overlapping and confusion.

On large building projects, where there may be a number of main contractors involved, it is desirable that there be coordination of public relations. It is very confusing to the press if announcements about the project are issued by a press officer working for a firm supplying some very minor service.

There are many opportunities in public relations for working together with other practitioners, and one of the benefits of membership of the International Public Relations Association, or a national public relations association, is the chance to meet and discuss mutual problems.

LIAISON WITH PARLIAMENT (LOBBYING)
It is desirable to know about the way in which the British Parliament

functions, for there are many occasions when liaison with Members of Parliament can assist in public relations projects. The special arrangements for the reporting of the proceedings of Parliament are described in the next chapter.

The importance of parliamentary liaison in industrial public relations varies according to the nature of an organisation's interests. If legislation is desired, or feared, obviously parliamentary work will be high in the list of priorities. In such cases, it will be wise to seek the help of a specialist who can advise on parliamentary procedure. Parliamentary agents come into the picture if it is desired to promote or oppose a Private Member's Bill.

There are a number of special groups in the House of Commons, composed of MPs with interest in a particular subject, eg transport, health or energy—and these can provide a means of meeting Members with a special interest in the organisation's views. In most cases there will be two parallel groups, one composed of Government supporters, the other from the Opposition. It may also be useful to find out which MPs will be willing to ask questions, or speak to a brief on some particular subject. It is not usually possible to do this except by meeting the Members and convincing them of the justice of the case you wish them to support.

Timing is all-important in this connection. Information which may be of little or no interest to Members at one moment—except perhaps in the case of one or two specialists—may be sought eagerly by them at another time, when for some reason it has become or is about to become topical in the parliamentary sense. It is necessary in dealing with Members of Parliament to put the right case, in the right way, at the right time.

Members receive a very large post daily—including, samples of shoddy goods, etc. Sometimes these tangible exhibits have been used to effect by Members when speaking in debate, but discretion should be exercised in this matter as Members' waste-paper baskets are not limitless!

When writing to MPs it is best to address the letters to the House of Commons, as the post office in the Palace of Westminster will forward correspondence if the Member is away; in fact, many MPs arrange for their secretaries to collect their letters daily from the House of Commons post office. When a matter is being considered by a standing committee, it is sometimes advisable to make a selective approach to the fifty or sixty members of the committee, rather than write to all MPs.

Personal contact is always the best way of establishing mutual respect, and many organisations invite Members of all parties to informal luncheons or dinner parties where matters of interest can be discussed 'off the record'.

The life of an MP is such a busy one that it is better for him to be approached by associations speaking for a number of companies than by single firms. Every company, however, and indeed every individual, has the right to discuss problems with Members of Parliament. In some instances, the chairman or managing director may decide to approach his own Member, for MPs often take more notice of the troubles or views of their own constituents.

Members of the House of Lords may have more time to listen to special pleading, and are usually keenly interested to hear about subjects which are of public interest or may be suitable for debating in the House of Lords. The legislative programme of the House of Commons is usually a crowded one, and it is sometimes useful for a matter to be raised first in the House of Lords where it can be fully ventilated—and possibly legislation set in motion which might not be possible to initiate in the House of Commons for many years.

For more details about liaison with Parliament, see *Parliamentary Lobbying* by Nigel Ellis. Heinemann September 1988.

The above relates to the Palace of Westminster, but increasingly it becomes desirable to consider lobbying at the European Commission in Brussels and at the Council of Europe in Strasbourg. This requires specialised experience and a number of agencies can be employed for this purpose.

TRADE ASSOCIATIONS

The activities of a trade association cover a very wide field in serving its members, but at least seventy-five per cent of its work falls within the field of public relations. It is often difficult to isolate the different aspects of an association of this kind, but a major part of its function is to create understanding and foster cooperation between its members, and to serve as a bridge between them and the outside world.

It is impossible to generalise about these associations. In the United Kingdom they number more than two thousand, and range from rich, influential bodies like the Society of Motor Manufacturers and Traders down to small little-known bodies which exist to serve a highly specialised section of an industry. All these bodies practise public relations, some as part of their management, others through a separate department. In some instances a small association carries out an ambitious public relations programme on behalf of its members, who provide the funds by a levy. Most large associations have found it satisfactory to have their own internal public relations department, but a small association would find it more practical to employ an outside consultant. It is not possible for the secretary, or his deputy when there is one, to maintain a sustained level of public relations activities in addition to his other manifold duties, and in most instances these senior executives lack the experience or the public relations outlook essential for success in this field.

The following are some of the public relations activities that are likely to be carried out by associations:

1 Acting as spokesman for the members, or their industry, and representing their interests on official and semi-official committees and in negotiations with Government departments.

2 Carrying out statistical and other forms of research, and providing an information service for the press, for members, and for others interested in the industry.

3 Organising collective displays, demonstrations and exhibitions; and holding conferences and meetings.

4 Providing export information and giving advice on overseas markets.

5 Publishing journals, bulletins, reports, etc, both for the private use of members and for informing outside opinion on the activities of the industry.

6 Making films, or seeking other forms of publicity, to further the interests of the members of the association, eg by encouraging new entrants to the industry.

It is usual to have as president of the association an outstanding person who should be willing to speak in public about the association's aims and objects.

This is a good opportunity to repeat that public relations can never be a substitute for correct policies. A trade association once asked for a public relations service to be provided by a consultant. This particular trade was at that time not in favour with the public. The consultant looked into the activities of the members of the association, and came to the conclusion that they were in the main giving an indifferent service and charging too much. He reported this to the association, and advised them that until their members changed their ways there was nothing to be gained by publicising them.

The common belief is that trade associations exist to maintain high prices, and that their actions are mainly inimical to general public interest. This mistaken opinion springs from the failure of trade associations to explain their function more clearly to the public. Indeed, in many instances even members of an association have only a very vague idea of its activities.

Members should keep in close touch with their trade association, which is the natural repository of an industry's latest information, achievements and problems.

The Trade Association's Strength as a Public Relations Agency

Public relations carried out by a trade association on behalf of its members has an authority that is often lacking when done by individual companies, for the following reasons:

1 The association can speak for a whole industry and therefore with detachment, balance and accuracy.

2 The views and help of trade associations are often sought by newspapers and broadcasting authorities, which might consider that the views of an individual company are more likely to be coloured by self-interest.

3 A big trade association has the finance and resources to plan group activities for an industry, such as films, exhibitions, etc.

Professional Associations and Scientific Bodies

A professional association is composed of individuals as members, in contrast to a trade association which usually has limited companies as its members. This difference induces a different emphasis, but in general all that has been said about the need for public relations in trade associations applies equally in the case of professional bodies. Often the need is greater, for professional people often appear to like secrecy for secrecy's sake when a more enlightened attitude would be to their own advantage. Anyone who has carried out public relations activities for professional bodies can testify to the frustration often engendered by indifference to public opinion and by an ingrained desire for secrecy.

The same attitude prevails in scientific bodies, but with more justification. Scientific progress is usually a slow and continuing process, and premature disclosure of results—or wild claims—can be very embarrassing for all concerned. Even when new discoveries have been made, the scientists like to wait until time has shown the value of the new ideas beyond all doubt.

Nevertheless, science cannot prosper without the sympathy of public opinion, and many leading scientists have broken down the old barriers and have taken positive steps to keep the public informed on new developments. Radio and television have made a notable contribution in this respect.

This enlightenment is spreading slowly to scientific bodies in general, and there is a growing willingness to adopt public relations ideas in order to win public understanding and goodwill which is so helpful to the achievement of their objectives. But there is still a need for scientific bodies to use modern methods of mass communication to inform the public of the meaning of scientific advances. There is an equally great need to attract the required numbers, and quality, of young men and women into scientific occupations.

Professions such as architects, solicitors and accountants are now allowed in the UK to advertise and use public relations services.

PUBLIC RELATIONS IN SUPPORT OF EXPORTS
Public relations can assist companies to enlarge the scope of their overseas activities. Organised public relations will facilitate the establishment and maintenance of advantageous business relations, and can be used in direct support of all types of marketing effort.

Competition in overseas markets is so keen that it is not sufficient to be able to supply the right goods at the right price and to be able to give reasonably good delivery. Direct advertising has an important part to play in support of overseas sales campaigns, but its effect will be enhanced if public opinion in the territory concerned is being cultivated by organised public relations methods.

The aim of public relations programmes directed at overseas

targets is first to protect the general reputation of goods and services, and secondly to enhance the reputation of the goods supplied by a particular company or industry. It might appear that only the second of these objectives is the concern of individual exporters, but unless the general reputation of a country's goods and services stands high, it will be difficult for individual exporters to extend their overseas activities. The British Government accepts responsibility for general publicity overseas in support of British industry.

The Advantages of Cooperation

Many trade associations do excellent public relations work overseas on behalf of their members, and this is a service that should be given high priority. Manufacturers should give these cooperative efforts their whole-hearted support, for through them excellent results can be achieved for relatively small *per capita* expenditure. Cooperative public relations programmes demand little from the individual manufacturer except financial support, but the implementation by an individual exporter of overseas public relations needs much greater organisation and the use of professional help.

Local Knowledge is Essential

It is seldom possible for a national of one country to be fully familiar with the nuances of public opinion and the complexity of communication media in other countries, and this type of knowledge is the essential raw material on which a successful public relations campaign must be based. It will therefore be necessary in most instances to seek professional public relations assistance in the overseas territory concerned. Many reputable public relations consultancies in the United Kingdom have close links with similarly experienced public relations organisations in the major territories and industrial centres of the world. An advantage of using the services of one of the internationally linked groups is that a campaign can be directed from the home country but serviced by nationals in the overseas countries concerned.

The extent to which the various media of public relations will feature in any overseas campaign will depend on the particular territory and on the nature of the product or service to be exported. It is in assessing the existing conditions, advising on the choice of suitable media, and preparing and disseminating appropriate material, that experienced public relations practitioners can assist exporters to secure the best results from available resources. There is no substitute, however, for personal reconnaissance visits to the area concerned.

London is one of the world's main news centres, and most newspapers and periodicals have representatives resident in the United Kingdom. It is obviously good policy to maintain contact with these foreign correspondents and to give them every opportunity for securing news to wire home.

Not many other countries have the abundance of good trade and technical journals that British people take so much for granted and many of these periodicals have an important overseas circulation, and provide a useful medium of public relations—especially in the technical field.

Radio and television have a powerful mass appeal, especially in the developing countries, and industrial films made with television in mind can achieve a wide showing on their screens.

Speaking in the Right Language

Even between countries supposedly speaking the same language, such as the United Kingdom and the United States, it is necessary to ascertain that the correct choice of words is made, both to ensure clarity of meaning and to avoid the possibility of giving offence. This problem of language becomes much greater when dealing with Latin America, the Soviet Union, Japan and other countries where English is not universally understood. Even in countries where a very high proportion of the population speak and understand English (such as Holland and Scandinavia) it is essential to use the local language correctly in publicity. It is reported that certain types of consumer goods sell well in Western Europe through advertising in English and using packs printed in English. This is due presumably to a kind of snob appeal which does not usually have a similar effect in public relations activities designed to inform and persuade.

The necessity of using the appropriate language for publications, exhibition captions, press releases, etc, is obvious; the difficulty comes in securing thoroughly satisfactory translations. It is not always possible to get the translation done in the country where it is to be used, as this may take too long; but it is wise to get the translation made by a national of the country concerned. There is little difficulty with the more widely-spoken languages, but if trouble is experienced in obtaining a translator for some of the less common ones, it is often possible to obtain help from the staff of the BBC External Services.

If the subject matter is of a technical or specialised nature, it is also necessary to make sure that the translator knows the subject exhaustively and is cognisant of new developments. Most people can recall sad experiences when translations have been made by willing persons lacking the necessary technical background. Whenever time permits it is wise to send a copy of the translation for checking in the country concerned.

It is not possible to over-emphasise the need for accurate translations, as mis-spelling, bad grammar and the use of obscure idiom create a very bad impression at the receiving end. There is an opportunity here for trade associations and bodies like chambers of commerce to help their members.

EIBIS International is a commercial organisation which will translate and distribute news stories or technical articles to a very wide selection of overseas journals (3 Johnson's Court, London EC4B 4HH).

The Universal News Services provides a UK wire service and also translates and distributes news stories to international media (Communications House, Gough Square, London EC4P 4DP).

It is helpful to take the trouble to learn something about local likes and dislikes, and to respect rivalries between neighbouring cities or regions. One example is the keen rivalry in Australia between Sydney and Melbourne, and similar rivalry exists between many other neighbouring cities. Reading the local newspapers is usually helpful in gaining an understanding of local conditions and providing topics for conversation.

It is necessary to learn and use the correct names of countries. Too many letters are still sent to Africa, South East Asia and other parts of the world wrongly addressed, and this often causes great offence. Above all, it is essential to remember that airmail exists, and not to send important letters by surface mail.

Body Language

An advertising campaign by BAA (formerly the British Airports Authority) emphasises the importance of body language. Harmless gestures or movements which are acceptable in one culture can give offence to others. This is not significant in the ordinary way but great care is necessary when exhibiting or sending printed matter to certain countries.

Overseas Visits by Businessmen
The companies which do well in exporting are usually those whose senior executives make frequent visits overseas. These visits are made primarily for business purposes, but if those concerned are willing to give talks to local societies, appear on radio and TV, and give interviews to the local press, their visits can benefit national prestige as well as fostering the businessmen's own particular interests. The planning of talks, press conferences, etc, on the spot is very much a public relations matter, and specialist advice should be sought.

In Britain, the Department of Trade and Industry gives financial assistance to approved outward and inward trade missions organised by non-profit-making bodies such as trade associations or chambers of commerce. This has been most useful in encouraging a greater two-way flow of experts and buyers—which can be a major factor in promoting increased exports.

SPONSORSHIP
Sponsorship is the modern development of patronage. In earlier times, monarchs and the nobility were the patrons of the arts but gradually this function was taken over by the state, even though it was on a reasonably limited scale. During the last few years, however, industry has taken an increasing interest in sponsorship of the arts and sport.

Industry sponsorship has a more direct benefit ratio than its predecessor, philanthropy. Rockefeller and Carnegie were examples of American millionaires who perpetuated their names by generous philanthropy. In Britain, colleges and universities have been endowed by Nuffield, Wolfson and others and there are a number of foundations which give grants to a wide variety of deserving causes. Sponsorship is on a smaller scale but its commercial benefits are more in direct ratio to effort and expenditure.

A useful definition of *sponsorship* is that it is essentially a business deal intended to be to the advantage of both the sponsor and the sponsored. Although sometimes funded from advertising budgets, it should be regarded as an entirely separate element of marketing.

Sponsorship is part of the marketing-mix which has a direct effect on the corporate identity of a company so the public relations aspect is important and sponsorship should be integrated with the public relations policies.

The sponsored activity may or may not be closely linked to the prime commercial function of the sponsoring organisation. On the other hand:

Patronage is fundamentally an altruistic activity;

Subsidy is aid from national or local government sources;

Endorsement is payment in return for the agreed use of specific equipment or clothing.

Sponsorship differs from the other types of support in that it is providing resources in return for expected benefit of a direct nature.

There are many different forms of sponsorship in current use:

1   *Sport.* The largest proportion of sponsors' money goes into sport. This includes cricket, snooker, tennis, motor racing, show jumping, golf, swimming, cycle racing, athletics and almost every other sport.

2   The second most important branch of sponsorship is *Arts* and *Culture*. This ranges from support for opera, concerts, the theatre and ballet to individual artistic events.

3   *Books* are a favourite form of sponsorship. The Michelin Guide and the Guinness Book of Records are two well-known examples.

4   *Exhibitions* are one of the older examples of sponsorship. The Daily Mail Ideal Home Exhibition has been running successfully in London for many years.

5   *Education.* Sponsored scholarships, chairs at university, research projects and industrial bursaries are examples of assistance in the higher educational field. Primary and secondary schools are also pleased to receive information packs and resource materials provided the advertising element is minimal.

6   *Professional awards.* Many sponsored awards are given for proficiency in journalism, architecture, the theatre, management and a range of other worthwhile activities.

7   *Charities and Good Causes.*

8 *Expeditions.* These range from supporting the first ascent of Everest to giving financial help to many expeditions and feats of exploration.

9 *Local events.* Flower shows, carnivals and swimming galas are examples of local sponsorship which has been running successfully for years—a very early example of industrial sponsorship.

COLLECTIVE SPONSORSHIP

A new development in sponsorship is the idea of bringing together a group of non-competitive companies to share the sponsorship of a major sports event like the Davis Cup. The main sponsor of the Davis Cup (for international tennis) is now the Nippon Electric Company (NEC).

NEC's reason for sponsoring the Davis Cup was essentially of a public relations nature. The company is one the world's leaders in communication technology and one of the least known. NEC was seeking name exposure and it was also looking for an international, respected platform. It wanted to gain recognition as an important company in its own right.

NEC wished to be seen clearly as associated with the Davis Cup so at every tie it has sponsor boards on court, identification on the umpire's chair and so on. The letters NEC are incorporated into the official logo and title, appearing on all programmes and other official literature. It is also involved in press activities, hospitality, entertainment and special publications.

The collective sponsorship scheme applies to the Davis Cup with a number of other sponsors taking part in all the ties and supporting events. Coca-Cola has coolers on every Davis Cup Court. Lacoste, the sports goods and clothing manufacturers, and Iveco, truck and bus manufacturers, who provide special transport, benefit from consistent exposure which is relevant to their own activity.

A different type of sponsorship is the 'Live Music Now' Foundation set up by the world famous violinist, Sir Yehudi Menuhin. The first event of this foundation in France was a concert by Menuhin for the staff of the Pernod Company at their works at La Pernoderie. The success of this concert led to the formation of the 'Presence de la Musique' based on the British 'Live Music Now'. 'The Presence de la Musique'—sponsored by Pernod and other French companies—gives between 100 and 200 concerts each year in schools, hospitals, barracks and prisons.

A spectacular goodwill sponsorship is that of Goodyear with its airships in Europe and the USA. On the one hand this furthers research into this form of aviation, but the airships also provide aerial platforms for television crews filming sports events, or help with traffic control. At night, the airships have flown over cities with public service messages illuminated electronically on their sides.

There is little doubt that sponsorship will grow in importance and remain one of the important aspects of public relations.

13 Central Government

Public relations is an essential part of management, and this is as true in central government as in industry. The function of public relations in government is essentially non-political. Political parties organise public relations to publicise or promote their party's policy and candidates. Public relations in a government department has two main tasks: to give regular information on policy, plans and achievements of the department; and to inform and educate the public on legislation, regulations and all matters that affect the daily life of citizens. It must also advise Ministers and senior officials of reaction and potential reaction to current or proposed policies.

The advantage of having an efficient public relations service in central government has become generally accepted, and is found today in most government departments. The duties of public relations divisions vary somewhat, and so do the names. For example, the Ministry of Defence has a Chief of Public Relations; the Treasury has a Press Secretary and Head of Information Division; while in other departments the information set-up may be headed by an officer variously styled Director of Information, Head of Information Division, or Chief Information Officer. All these posts, however, carry status and salary broadly similar to an Assistant Secretary.

In most segments of government ministries, the public relations division has an opportunity of expressing an opinion in discussions at all levels, and the head of the division enjoys the full confidence of his minister and the senior officials of the department. It is recognised that he cannot fulfil his duties without access to full information, and that he should be consulted when policy is being formulated.

The Organisation of Government Information Services

In the United Kingdom, each Minister is responsible for the public relations policy of his own department. About thirty government departments have public relations divisions. They maintain relations with the press and the broadcasting services, and also plan the publicity output of their departments. For the actual production of publicity material and for technical advice they look in general to the Central Office of Information (COI) which is a specialised common service organisation.

The COI is organised on a craft basis, so that experts are available in every sphere. The alternative would be for each Ministry to have its own specialists—which would be costly, even if sufficient experts were available. There would also be limited scope for promotion within a Ministry.

The COI supplies departments with technical publicity advice, maintains a number of distributive services which they need in common, and produces finished material such as films, press services, photographs, publications and exhibitions, all of which are backed by a reference service. The COI has its own budget and presents its own account to Parliament, but virtually the whole of its expenditure is incurred in carrying out work for which other departments have asked and for which they take the final policy responsibility.

The only major distinction between the relations which the COI has with the Foreign and Commonwealth Office as compared to the home departments lies in the fact that the COI does not itself employ staff in overseas countries. In Britain, the COI does not merely produce material but is often also responsible for the organisation of its use, which in overseas countries is the responsibility of the field staff of the Diplomatic Service.

The staff working in government public relations are drawn from the Information Officer Class, a general service class of the Civil Service which first came into existence in 1949. This has been accepted by all departments other than the Foreign and Commonwealth Office.

Coordination of Services

Although each department is responsible for its own information policy, there will clearly be some issues which concern several departments. It is also necessary to ensure that departments plan their information work in full knowledge of overall government strategy and the activities of other departments, so that duplication in effort and timing is avoided. Successive administrations have therefore charged a Minister with the responsibility of securing sufficient coordination of information work at this level. At present the Home Secretary, assisted by one of the two Parliamentary Secretaries to the Civil Service Department, is generally responsible for the government's information services. At the official level the coordination of the departmental information effort has been placed by the Prime Minister in the charge of the Chief Press Secretary, and is organised through a series of regular and *ad hoc* meetings chaired by the Chief Press Secretary or his staff. Questions on overseas information services are answered by the Parliamentary Under Secretary of State for Foreign Affairs.

The Organisation of a Government Public Relations Department

The internal arrangement of a department will depend on the relative importance of the different aspects of the work, and the accent will vary substantially between different Ministries. It is usual, however, for there to be four sub-divisions: the press office, the television and broadcasting section, the publicity section, and the intelligence or briefing section.

Many Ministries have public inquiry rooms, and these may be the responsibility of the public relations department; but the practice differs on this point. Whether they are directly concerned with such information rooms or not, the public relations staff will be involved in their operation in many different ways.

Press Relations

Press relations forms a large part of government public relations, and it is beset by many complications not generally found in press relations work. The press office supplies news and explanation to the newspapers, magazines, specialist journals, and to the overseas departments for use abroad. Distribution is usually through the COI by teleprinter or vans. The regional offices of the COI also distribute press material from the departments to the regional press.

The press office staff need specialist knowledge of how to deal with (*a*) debates in Parliament—major debates or adjournment debates; (*b*) documents of the House such as White Papers, Reports, Bills, etc; (*c*) statements by Ministers; (*d*) question time in the House, not forgetting supplementaries.

Parliament is served by two groups of journalists: the Parliamentary Press Gallery and the Lobby. The former have the task of reporting the actual proceedings of Parliament—what is said in the two Houses, and what occurs there. The Lobby correspondents have the unique privilege of entering the Inner Lobby of the House and of freely mingling there with Members of Parliament and Ministers. Their task is to obtain the background to events and to write for their papers on the policy and purpose of the Government's proposals and the Opposition's reactions. The Lobby has its own meeting room in the House where it holds meetings to which Ministers are invited to come and discuss matters with the Lobby.

Parliament is jealous of its privileges, but has allowed the members of the Lobby certain facilities in the knowledge that they will not be abused. The Lobby has a restricted membership, and even national Sunday newspapers do not have a permanent seat but are allowed to come one day a week. Foreign papers are also fully represented in the Press Gallery but not in the Lobby. Regular press conferences are held at No 10 Downing Street, where spokesmen give official views and comment on the topics of the day.

A departmental press office receives inquiries from United Kingdom newspapers and also from London correspondents of the overseas press, and it is important that arrangements be made to deal with these inquiries adequately, by day and by night. When the department has legislation before Parliament, or other special events are taking place, the stream of inquiries may become a flood and special arrangements may be necessary. The manner in which Government departments deal with press inquiries varies considerably: some press offices provide an excellent service, others not so good!

The press office also arranges press visits to Government establishments, and organises press conferences at which Ministers or senior officials make statements and answer questions. Such press conferences are similar to other press conferences described in Chapter 3.

Television and Broadcasting Section

The growing importance of television and broadcasting as information media has led to the setting up of a press and broadcasting section separate from the press office which hitherto served both press and broadcasting. The functions of the two sections are essentially the same, but the different nature of the two media means that they require different facilities.

Publicity Services

The publicity section concerns itself mainly with films, posters, leaflets, press advertising and other paid-for material. It works in cooperation with local authorities, other government departments, and the Central Office of Information (COI). When a department has an important message which ought to reach people throughout the country, it may not be enough to make use of the free media of publicity. Paid-for publicity and advertising make it possible to repeat information which does not keep its news value once it has been announced, and enables the department to present its message in full and in its own way. The Advisory Committee on Appointment of Advertising Agents, an outside independent body, advises the COI on the choice of advertising agencies for government campaigns.

Intelligence and Briefing Services

The fourth section of the department is usually an intelligence or briefing section which collects information about the department and its interests and feeds it to the press and publicity sections, and to the COI for use overseas.

The point has already been made in Chapter 1 that public relations is the responsibility of everyone in an organisation and is not the sole prerogative of the public relations staff. This is equally true in the Government service. The Minister, and indeed every civil servant, has his own contacts with the public and with authorities which are able to provide evidence of what people are doing and saying. The public relations officer can supply supplementary intelligence, and it is an important part of his duties to keep the rest of his department promptly informed on what is appearing in the press and what is being said and shown on radio and television. He should do more than this: he should try to ensure that public relations thinking is allowed to play a part in shaping all the policies of the Ministry for it is easier and more effective to govern a reasonably well-informed people.

The desirability of governing with the consent of the people concerned generally results in long and detailed discussions taking place with a wide variety of interested organisations and individuals before a Ministry issues a White Paper. The public relations officer will usually have had an opportunity of expressing an opinion on the wording of the White Paper and the timing of its publication, and will of course have the main task of publicising it.

Questions in the House of Commons reflect public interest, as also do the questions which men and women send to the various inquiry bureaux run by newspapers and magazines. These bureaux welcome help from a Ministry public relations department, and in rendering this assistance it is possible to keep in touch with current public anxieties and misunderstandings.

The Future of Public Relations in Government

The old arguments as to whether public relations officers are necessary in government departments rarely arise today. The have become an accepted part of the administrative machinery of government, serving successive Ministers and Governments impartially to the best of their ability. In the past it was suggested—particularly in certain sections of the press—that it was wrong to have experienced public relations officers in government, for if they did their work well it redounded to the credit of a particular Minister and a particular party. This is no more true of a public relations officer than it is of any other departmental officer. The problem is no different from that of every Private Secretary and Permanent Secretary. Years of experience have drawn a sharp line—Ministers know it, as well as their officers—between official information and party propaganda, between the departmental occasion and the political platform.

Most Ministries give their public relations staff the opportunity to make a useful contribution to the work of the department at all levels, but in a few cases there is still a tendency to regard them merely as press and information officers. The most encouraging sign is that public relations staff in the Government service are paid as well as, if not better than, their opposite numbers working in industry—evidence that there is a true realisation of their valuable role in modern administration.

Summary
Public relations in central and local government must be non-political. It is to promote democracy and informed citizenship through full information and *not* to advance the policy of any political party.

The description of central government public relations organisation given in this Chapter relates to current practice in the United Kingdom. In other countries, with different political systems, the details may vary considerably but the rationale should always be the same.

14 Local Government

People suddenly develop an interest in local affairs when controversies arise over things that directly affect them. The resultant outcry over such things calls attention to the need for better local public relations. Public relations, however, is not a fire brigade to be called in to douse a conflagration of public opinion; it is the means to inform and educate the electorate to play its proper part in local affairs.

Local government is a shared responsibility, requiring a working partnership between the public and elected or appointed officials. Public relations provides the most effective means of achieving this cooperation.

The main objective is to develop a greater civic consciousness and to encourage people to take an active interest in their local government. This manifests itself in a greater willingness to run for elected office and in a demand that local officials give citizens an account of their stewardship. Increased public interest in local government helps prevent rule by cliques—however well-intentioned—and aids elected officials in adopting a constructive attitude toward their responsibility.

Four Main Objectives of Public Relations in Local Government
There are four main objectives:

    1 To keep people informed of council policy and day-to-day activities.

2   To give the public an opportunity to express views on important new projects before final decisions are reached.

3   To enlighten people on the way in which the system of local government works, and to inform them of their rights and responsibilities

4   To promote a sense of civic pride.

There are a variety of reasons why councillors have resisted the introduction of public relations in their areas. It is a traditional characteristic of local authorities to be suspicious of new ideas unless they save money. Some fear that public relations would amount to propaganda in support of the policies of the ruling majority, undertaken at public expense. A third objection is that many councillors regard it as their prerogative to maintain liaison between the council and the public. Even when councillors are reasonably favourably disposed toward public relations, they fear that it will prove too costly. The opposition does not come entirely from the elected representatives, for some officials resent the introduction of public relations experts who might, they think, undermine their authority or, by stimulating criticism as well as interest, add to their difficulties.

It is not public relations that is resisted so strongly in local government, but rather organised public relations. This feeling springs from conviction that public relations needs neither men nor money; councillors will naturally know the needs of their constituents. The facts are sufficient proof of the fallacy of this reasoning, honestly believed though it is. Indeed, the need for organised public relations is greater and more clearly established in government—both central and local—than in any other field, for democracy cannot flourish in the face of an uninformed electorate.

Councillors cannot meet the need unaided. They find that the meetings of councils and committees take up much of their available time, and most of them have either a living to earn or a family to look after. Few councillors are able to master completely the complexity of local government, let alone find time to pass on their knowledge to a large electorate.

How it Works Today
The public relations section in local government is generally a small one, consisting of the public relations officer, one or more assistants,

and clerical staff. The public relations officer usually reports to the general purposes committee, or sometimes a special public relations committee or sub-committee, through the Clerk of the Council. The officer attends council meetings and committee meetings that have a particular bearing on his work or activities at the time. It is customary for them to have the right to attend all committee meetings; the ideal arrangement, however, is to have this right but to exercise it as seldom as possible, for too frequent attendance at meetings is bound to interfere with the efficient execution of the many tasks which require attention.

Local authorities have a duty to keep their own staff informed, particularly on matters which may have a direct bearing on them. It is also very important that members of an authority should be provided with information on all relevant matters. In both of these vital spheres, an efficient public relations unit within an authority can provide a comprehensive information service.

The most important single aspect of public relations will always be the personal contact between the members and officers of a local authority and the public they serve. If a person visits a town hall with a problem and is received with indifference or discourtesy, no amount of subsequent publicity will eradicate the unfortunate impression made. The first objective of public relations in local government should be, therefore, to do everything possible to break down the barriers to friendly relations between officials and the public. All contacts—whether in person, by letter, or by telephone—should be made as easy and courteous as possible. Some councils have induction courses for new employees which include lectures on public relations.

When a citizen goes to a town hall, it should be easy to find the required service or department. The design of such buildings often makes it difficult to place the various departments in any logical sequence—which is all the more reason why adequate signposting is essential. Directions of this kind—where they exist—are often ambiguous, or illegible to all save those possessed of exceptionally keen eyesight.

The work in a county council will be on a larger scale than in a small local council, but the principles and conditions of the work will be very similar. In both cases the public relations officer will attempt to work in close cooperation with the departmental heads.

Relations with the Media

The principles and practice of press relations, as discussed in Chapter 3, apply in general to local government. The local press is easily the most effective means of communication between a council and citizens and, therefore, it is desirable that everything possible should be done to establish and maintain good relations with local editors and their staffs in order that local affairs shall be reported as fully and as objectively, as possible. Many people scoff at local newspapers, but their influence in local affairs is often far greater than that of the national daily papers.

It was because of the importance of local affairs being reported fully in local papers that Parliament recognised the right of the press to attend council meetings of local authorities or equivalent bodies.

The press obtains its news of local authority affairs mainly from the agenda and reports of councils and committees. One disadvantage of this arrangement is that all the council news tends to be concentrated into one period of each month. Enlightened councils, however, take steps to ensure a steady flow of news to the press.

When a national paper unearths an alleged 'scandal', the public relations officer should offer full facilities to the press to investigate the true facts of the matter, which are often quite different from those in the first garbled report which a particular reporter has obtained. There are many opportunities for misunderstanding—especially in the field of housing, and the care of young and old people—and these are subjects charged with human emotion. If a 'scandal' really exists then it is right to have it ventilated, as this will help to encourage the council to take the necessary corrective action. The press is the watchdog over the rights of the citizen, and by and large performs this duty with zeal and discretion.

Relations with radio and television are not so continuous as those with the press, but their impact is usually more forceful. There are a number of documentary programmes on both radio and television which seek out controversial issues and try to analyse the causes and ventilate the problems. Sometimes these programmes take a subject such as housing, or education, which affect the country as a whole; on other occasions they investigate dissatisfaction in particular towns or districts. There is only one satisfactory way to deal with this matter, and that is by offering all possible facilities to the producers of the programmes and by trying to ensure that they see both sides of the question.

On the positive side, radio and television producers will always be interested to hear about any unusual or characteristic local activities which might form the basis of a feature programme or news report. Some of these activities may not rate national interest, but may fit very well into regional programmes.

The introduction of local radio and television stations has extended the range of media available to public relations staff working in local government.

Relations with Local Residents

There are many ways in which enlightened local authorities have established good relations with their ratepayers and other local residents, and have been able to enlist their help in making local government work. Unfortunately, few authorities employ all these methods—and some use none of them.

Information Centres

Conditions constantly arise in which men and women need guidance on their rights or responsibilities in connection with a wide variety of aspects of local government. Many authorities operate information bureaux which deal with inquiries made in person, by letter, or on the telephone. Such information centres perform a vital social service as well as a public relations function, and every local authority should have a central point at which inquiries can be dealt with expeditiously, efficiently, and, when necessary, in privacy.

The Printed Word

Taxpayers should not be dependent upon the press for all their information about local government activities. In most aspects of modern life it is customary to make an annual report to members or shareholders, and this need applies equally to local government. Each authority should render an account of its stewardship— annually, quarterly, or even monthly—so that all taxpayers know about local developments that affect them. The issue of such civic reports takes place in some areas and has proved its worth. This does not interfere in any way with the function of the local press, and indeed, newspapers usually welcome bulletins as an additional means of information.

Corporate Image

Councils are always looking at costs, but the desire for economy should not be allowed to debase the standard of printed material issued by councils. Good typography and printing cost no more than bad design, and here there is scope for public relations officers to persuade their colleagues in local government of the desirability of maintaining the highest possible standard in print design. This also applies to posters, notice boards, signs, exhibitions, and so on. Each authority should adopt a suitable house style so that all the council's productions are readily identifiable. This helps to establish a corporate image for the authority, which aids overall efficiency.

Exhibitions

In local affairs, where the population is concentrated within a defined area, exhibitions are a very effective medium of public relations.

When there is reason to justify a major celebration, a large-scale civic exhibition can be considered. Small-scale exhibitions, however, can fill the continuing need for the imparting of information on many diverse subjects such as planning, welfare, road safety, health and education.

Small exhibitions need not be costly, but ingenuity should be exercised to make the standard of presentation as high as possible. It is also important to ensure variety in the design, so that if the exhibitions are in the local library, for example, one exhibition should be clearly distinguishable from the succeeding one.

Cooperation between departments is desirable since the initial cost is the major part of a small exhibition. By a sharing arrangement, a number of government divisions or offices can use an exhibition in turn.

Points of vantage such as notice boards outside public libraries or town halls can be used for the display of information, photographs, and posters, and can be a very effective means of communication with the public if used with imagination. Such notice boards need maintenance and regular cleaning.

Meetings and Lectures

The popularity of television has tended to reduce attendance at meetings of local societies and organisations, but these still remain one of the most effective methods of contact with influential people in the area. There is here an opportunity for a two-way flow of public relations: information can be disseminated through these organisations, and equally the views of their members can help to inform the council on public reaction to current issues. A public relations officer should consider it part of his duties to maintain the closest possible liaison with local bodies of all kinds.

Lectures to schools are an obvious way of interesting the future taxpayers, and such lectures come to life if they can be followed up by organised visits to different departments of an authority. NALGO pioneered two ideas in this connection which have proved very successful. The 'Inter-Schools Quiz' is a contest, leading to an area final, between teams of schoolchildren who have to answer questions on civic affairs. Its value is threefold: it encourages schools to include civic affairs in the teaching curriculum; it interests young people in local affairs; and, by attracting their parents to the contests, spreads the interest among their elders also. The second idea affects slightly older people. The 'Welcome to Citizenship' scheme is an annual reception given by a council to all the young men and women in the area who have reached the age of eighteen during the past year and have thus qualified for a municipal vote. The 'new' citizens are welcomed by the Mayor, councillors and chief officers, shown round the town hall and told how the council works. Finally, each is given a certificate, signed by the Mayor and Town Clerk, in recognition that he or she is now a fully-fledged citizen of the town. This simple ceremony, repeated year by year with each group of new voters, has achieved a good response from the young people involved, giving them a clearer idea of their personal share in democratic government and encouraging them to take an active part in local affairs. Many local authorities have adopted the scheme.

Summary

The arena of local affairs provides an obvious place for the function of public relations in almost all its aspects. Where organised public relations has been allowed to show its full potential, the results have been acclaimed as very successful; where local suspicion or prejudice has prevented its operation, an important and worthwhile job remains to be done. The effective way is to appoint skilled public relations staff with the resources to meet the needs of the area. This is not enough in itself: every member of a local council and its administration must be kept aware of the need to follow the principles of public relations and to build up mutual confidence.

No mention has been made in this chapter of holiday resort publicity or industrial development, which are sometimes included in the responsibilities of the public relations department. Where a public relations officer has duties in these fields, they should not be allowed to interfere with his primary task of making local government live in the mind of every citizen.

Confidentiality

In nearly all aspects of public relations, confidentiality is very important and practitioners are bound by the codes of professional conduct in this respect. Confidentiality is particularly important when working in central or local government.

15 Non-commercial fields

There are many public relations activities that affect the general well-being of the population and which are divorced from ordinary commercial implications. This social aspect is the main link between the activities considered in this chapter.

In the United States every sphere of communal life has its public relations advisers: schools, universities, public libraries, the churches, the police, public utilities, and so on. In the United Kingdom the initial interest came mainly from government and industry, with the community slow to follow.

Community relations is a very broad subject. Many aspects of community relations have already been discussed in Chapters 12 and 14 dealing with the private business sector and with local government. The primary mission of community relations is to develop or maintain mutual understanding.

Fund Raising

Fund raising is an important part of public relations, along with the special event planning necessary to raise funds and to express appreciation to those who have contributed.

The medical field is, of course, by no means the only sphere where fund raising has become essential. So much so, that fund raising has become a professional activity in itself. In the UK there have been some remarkably successful campaigns for the restoration of cathedrals. Recently a major success was achieved by the Great Ormond Street Hospital for Children.

Safeguarding the Environment

The public judges organisations by the way in which they behave, in the same way that individuals form good or bad impressions of people with whom they come into contact. Most large organisations are aware of the need to preserve the environment, and the electricity and oil companies, for example, go to considerable lengths to try to make new buildings and exposed plant blend into the surrounding countryside and obtrude as little as possible into local life. Any new industrial project, however, may interfere with local amenities, and great care should be taken to avoid pollution of the environment in any way.

Industry in the Community

A company with a large factory in a town is a source of wealth, both directly as tax revenue and through salaries paid to employees, and indirectly by stimulating other enterprises. The company will, of course, need to recruit labour locally, and there are many other ways in which it can be of great community assistance.

The need to play a part in local community affairs is now generally accepted by industry, and this may take a number of forms. It has become common practice for senior members of the firm to take an interest in local politics, and it is good policy to make it equally possible for workers to serve on local councils or boards.

A large company is usually in a position to give financial help to local charities and local projects such as youth clubs, athletic programmes and repertory theatres. In some cases, firms donate public parks, meeting halls, and the like. This kind of participation in local affairs does much to establish a company as a good neighbour and a desirable employer. Where a high proportion of the local people work for a company, it is obviously desirable for that company to support local activities generously; but this is equally well worth a company's involvement when the labour force is comparatively small.

Consumerism and Protests

The United States experienced the first stirrings of consumerism—the recognition that the interests of the consumer were of major importance. This movement has spread to Europe and many other parts of the world. Side by side with the growth of interest in consumerism has been a considerable increase in protest movements.

It has become fashionable for individuals or groups, aggrieved by events or proposed developments, to organise themselves in order to protest as effectively as possible. Their protests range from quiet peaceful manifestations to sometimes violent eruptions.

The main difference between protests and professional public relations practice is that protests are usually organised by amateurs—although sometimes with professional assistance—and are limited in time scale, while public relations practice is characterised by its continuing nature.

The enthusiasm engendered by the sense of grievance of those concerned gives considerable impetus to protests, and many such campaigns have succeeded in achieving their goals. However, a protest tends to be a volcano that erupts suddenly but may soon be forgotten unless it achieves positive results.

Protests exploit all the usual forms of public relations methods and cover all media. Political activity at local and/or national level is usually an essential element in a protest campaign.

Welcoming Visitors

Military establishments have set a good example to industry in hosting visiting days, special tours, exhibits, demonstrations, and shows as ways of securing public interest and cooperation. The military learned long ago that one of the most effective ways of establishing good community relations was by opening the doors to their ships or military establishments as often as practicable.

A number of industrial companies in various fields have welcomed visitors to their factories for many years and have been well satisfied with the results. The practice of inviting organised parties has spread, and some companies will show any visitor around their factories even without prior appointment. Evening visits may be a good idea in certain cases, as they permit family participation.

In some industries, the entertaining of visitors tends to interfere with production, and for this reason such factories prefer to hold open houses each year to which employees can bring their relatives, and when local residents and other people likely to be interested can also visit.

It is important to make suitable arrangements to receive visitors: This entails not only the provision of trained guides, but also of amenities such as adequate rest rooms. Security and safety require special attention.

After a suitable welcome, parties should be split up into small groups, each under a guide. The guides should have received adequate training so that they carry out their duties satisfactorily. In addition to having extensive knowledge of a company and its processes, guides need a sense of loyalty to the organisation—and positive measures should be taken to maintain their enthusiasm. Among ways of doing this are:

1   Promising that the best guides will be selected to guide VIP parties, and giving those guides an extra fee for this.

2   Holding discussion groups at which guides can meet factory managers and hear about new developments and company policy.

3   Sending guides occasionally to visit other factories as members of ordinary visiting parties, so that they can see how others do it or learn some of the things not to do.

It is usual to offer some refreshments to organised visiting parties; for morning visits coffee or tea and biscuits will probably be adequate, while in the afternoon soft drinks, sandwiches, or cake will be suitable. Refreshments are usually offered at the end of a conducted tour, but if a factory is in an isolated location and parties have travelled some distance, it may be preferable to serve refreshments first or as a break during the tour. Souvenirs are usually provided for visitors, and are appreciated even if it is only printed material about the organisation. Company products like chocolate or beer are always appreciated.

Voluntary or Non-Profit Organisations

There are thousands of voluntary or non-profit organisations in every country and most of them face the constant need to raise funds. But whereas in some instances this is the main object of the organisation, in other cases the money is needed for the pursuance of social work, youth welfare, and other worthy causes.

The running of a large voluntary organisation of any kind is itself a continuing exercise in public relations. Since the majority of the workers—both at headquarters and in widely dispersed branches—

are unpaid, it is necessary to maintain their interest at a high pitch by keeping them in sympathy with the aims of the organisation and by retaining their confidence in headquarters' policy and efficiency. Assuming that the policy of the organisation is right, this resolves itself mainly into a problem of communication.

The internal communications are usually in writing and by personal contact between the officials and the branches and the members. Without incurring undue expense, it is always possible to improve the house journal—or to start one—and to modernise circulars, publicity leaflets, letterheads, and so on. Personal contacts are even more important, and the guiding principle should be to make them as frequent as possible.

The public image of a voluntary organisation is very important to its success both in attracting financial support and in securing the willing cooperation of voluntary workers. It is necessary to show clearly that the organisation deserves support and that it is performing a function which the state cannot—or will not—perform adequately, and which is not being done by other bodies.

It is clear that voluntary organisations need expert public relations advice, since their efficiency can be improved by the adoption of appropriate techniques. While there are special occasions when public relations men and women should give voluntary help, in general voluntary bodies should be prepared to appoint experienced public relations officials to their headquarters staff or to use the services of consultants. Unfortunately, the committees of voluntary bodies often include a high proportion of men and women who have no practical business experience and who mistrust advertising or public relations. These people are inclined to resist any suggestion of spending money on anything as intangible as public relations. It is necessary, therefore, to explain how it can contribute to the success of the organisation, and to show that public relations is as real as print, films, talks, and other accepted means of communication, which are, indeed, its very essence.

When the headquarters of a voluntary organisation has adopted a progressive public relations programme, the next step is to see that this policy is also implemented throughout the organisation. Lectures on public relations should be given to local branches as opportunity permits, and committees encouraged to make someone responsible for liaison with the local media.

INTERNATIONAL ORGANISATIONS

The activities of the United Nations Organisation are primarily political, but there are many associated bodies such as Unesco and the World Health Organisation whose activities have a profound effect on world educational cooperation.

The success of any international project depends on the pursuance of correct public relations policies, for it is necessary to secure and maintain the support of peoples of varying cultural, religious, and political beliefs.

Public relations for an international organisation presents similar problems to those met in other branches of the work, but the canvas is so much wider that policies and techniques have to be adjusted accordingly. The public relations staff will be recruited from different nationalities to avoid any national bias, and this helps to overcome the main difficulty of planning to meet the requirements of different areas.

The main media of public relations used within this field are publications, press and films, and the holding of conferences, study groups, and so forth. Most international organisations are doing excellent work in these fields, but there is almost unlimited scope for extending the activities, limited in fact only by available finance.

The International Public Relations Association is one of many Non-Governmental Organisations which are recognised by the United Nations as valuable partners. IPRA's recognition by the United Nations Economic and Social Council dates from 1974 and IPRA has Consultative Status, Category B, with Unesco.

16 Case Histories

The best way to understand and appreciate public relations practice is by examining actual cases. There are a number of excellent books which discuss case studies in depth, explaining the problem or challenge, describing the programme and assessing the results.

In this volume, which sets out to 'introduce' the concept and practice of public relations, it is not possible to give case studies in depth but the following examples will illustrate the wide range of public relations in action.

Bricks and Mortar Public Relations

An outstanding public relations success started as 'Rockefeller's Folly'. This was the name given in the early thirties to the ambitious scheme started by the late John D Rockefeller, Jr in the heart of New York City. This early example of urban renewal was started during the Depression, and roused great criticisms from architects and city planners alike. They complained that the architecture was undistinguished and the project had no civic purpose. Rockefeller kept quiet about the fact that he had originally leased the dozen acres on Fifth Avenue (between 48th and 51st Street) on behalf of a group planning a new home for the Metropolitan Opera, and that when the other backers had withdrawn after the 1929 crash he was left with this huge liability.

Unmoved by the criticism, Rockefeller pressed on with his plans for a modern city development that would be something new in city planning. He personally supervised construction work on the Center, and one day while he was standing on the pavement watching a huge steam shovel in an excavation a guard tapped him on the shoulder and told him to move on. Rockefeller moved on, but as a result of this experience he had windows cut in the high board walls around the site so that passersby could stop and watch the excavation work. The idea proved so popular that the Center's public relations department formed the Sidewalk Superintendents' Club, printed membership cards, and handed them out to the assembled watchers.

Financially speaking, the Rockefeller Center made a bad start, but now, more than 50 years later, this has long been forgotten and the Center, further expanded, is both a financial success and a tourist mecca. Each day it is visited by more than 200,000 employees and visitors who enjoy its flower gardens, rest on its seats, watch skaters on its outdoor ice rink, and generally treat its handsome plaza as if it were a village square. Many New Yorkers believe that the plaza is city property, whereas it is a private street.

The success of the Rockefeller Center has encouraged ambitious urban renewal schemes in many other American cities and these schemes owe much to Rockefeller's initial boldness in contributing a new concept to modern city development. This must surely rank high as an example of community public relations.

Combatting Rumours 1

Procter & Gamble, one of the United States' largest manufacturers with annual sales of more than $11 billion, ran into an unusual problem with the symbol that the company has used as a trademark since 1851. The circular symbol represents the man-in-the-moon with 13 stars representing the original 13 colonies in the United States. The man-in-the-moon was a popular symbol at the time the trademark was established.

Somehow a rumour started in the western United States that the firm's 131-year-old corporate symbol shows sympathy for the devil. Suddenly the firm began receiving hundreds of calls and letters from people who claimed they had either seen a corporate executive on a national television talk show relate that the symbol shows the company's ties to the worship of Satan or had been told the information at their church.

In addition to responding to the inquiries with the facts, Procter & Gamble began an aggressive programme that included sending letters to every newspaper, television, and radio station in the localities where the rumour had spread. In addition regional and national church leaders of various denominations were contacted and their help sought in stopping the rumours. The Procter & Gamble mailings explained the origin of the crescent moon symbol and included a letter from the host of the national talk show explaining that no Procter & Gamble executive had ever appeared on his programme to discuss satanism.

Combatting Rumours 2

Early in 1981, the attention of Colgate-Palmolive (Malaysia) was drawn to reports (in a couple of newspapers) and allegations that pig fat was being used to manufacture Colgate toothpaste.

These rumours, which affected sales in some areas, were particularly strong in:

1   Certain rural communities.

2   Some schools, where headmasters and teachers were advising Muslim children to refrain from using Colgate toothpaste.

Indeed, a vicious whispering campaign to stop Muslims from using Colgate toothpaste was under way.

The Company's attention was also directed to circulars by officials of a few Government associations stating that it was 'un-Islamic' to use Colgate dental cream.

Seventeen people from various parts of the country wrote protest letters to the Company. A quick survey by Company officials showed that while the allegations were serious, the anti-Colgate movement was confined to small groups. Confrontation with these groups in the National Press was considered inadvisable. Why stir things up and spread the allegations?

So it was decided to take a discreet approach with a programme involving:

1   Talks to Muslim leaders.

2   Direct Mail to heads of Muslim schools.

3   Restricted publicity, with the assistance of the Islamic Press.

The Objective
To stop the rumours and educate 'non-believers' on the facts of Colgate dental cream.

The Action Plan
After a series of meetings between senior executives of the Company and its public relations consultants, it was decided to mount an exercise directed at those responsible for the allegation.

The following were chosen for attention:

1   Those who had complained directly to the Company.

2   Heads of 3,380 Malay schools who wield considerable influence in the rural areas.

Before contacting them, however, it was decided to strengthen the Company's case by inviting:

1   Officials from SIRIM (The Government's Standards Industrial Research Institute) to visit the Colgate plant and report on the contents of the toothpaste.

2   Senior journalists from two Islamic monthly magazines—Al Islam and Qiblat—to tour the plant and report on their findings.

The SIRIM Report entirely backed the Company and categorically stated there was 'no pig fat' in Colgate toothpaste.

The Journalists too concurred with SIRIM's findings and commented very favourably (in their magazines) on the product.

Direct Mail
A total of 13,000 copies of the magazines featuring the favourable articles were ordered. These, together with a circular letter (from the Company) and a self-addressed reply card—for feedback—were sent to:

1   3,380 heads of Malay schools.

2   17 individuals who had protested directly to the Company.

The rest of the magazines, letters and cards were distributed to the public through Colgate's sales outlets in the rural areas.

The reply card asked these questions:

1 Are you satisfied with the explanation given in the magazines and circular letter?

2 Would you like Colgate representatives to call on you for a dialogue?

3 Would you like to visit the Colgate plant—alone or in a group?

4 Do you have any comments?

Monitoring Progress
Only 36 per cent (or 1,205 people) responded to the 3,383 letters that were despatched. In view of this, a second direct mail exercise was mounted (enclosing the same materials) for the remaining 2,178 who had failed to respond.

Feedback from Direct Mail

Total number replied	1,269
Satisfied with explanation	2,048
Number requesting SIRIM report	1,539
Number wanting the meet Colgate representatives	78
Number wishing to visit plant	4
Those not convinced by the Company's explanations	169

Of the 17 who had complained directly to the Company, 12 said they were satisfied with Colgate's explanation. Two others were 'not pleased'.

Respondents made a number of suggestions ranging from a call for greater rapport between the Company and the Muslim community to plant tours for Muslim teachers. Several asked for donations of toothpaste for students.

All their suggestions were studied and appropriate follow-up action taken.

The Colgate programme followed sound public relations objectives and implementation. The rumours were quashed. The Company won many new friends, and things went back to normal.

In the consumer field, rumours can be very hurtful. One often wonders if they are spread by competitors. One well-known example was the rumour in the United States that Macdonalds were using earthworms instead of meat in their hamburgers.

The Woolly Bears' Picnic

One of the problems with handling public relations for a pest-control company is that of educating the public and encouraging them to take action. The public must be informed that products or services are available to deal with specific pests.

A plague of the 'woolly bear' grubs of the carpet beetle *(Anthrenas verbasci)* was reported by a local newspaper in England. Alarmed householders called a meeting to discuss the problem. After fruitless contact with the local public health department, the local Rentokil pest-control surveyor and products salesman were asked to help, and this alerted Rentokil to the public relations potential of the situation.

A public meeting was organised at which an entomologist from the company's laboratories addressed 200 people, followed by questions and discussion lasting two hours. A local television crew then interviewed the entomologist, filmed a photogenic housewife/secretary using Rentokil spraying and dusting equipment, and even obtained film of the grubs themselves.

Later, network television conducted an interview, and the following day most national daily and major provincial newspapers gave the problem coverage. BBC Radio London and Radio Manchester recorded items on the subject, and *Practical Householder* and *Do-It-Yourself* both published short articles.

The effect was an increase in carpet beetle treatments all over England. Massive sales of Rentokil products resulted, and six times more mothproofer was sold than in the same period of the previous year—completely exhausting the factory's stock.

Apart from increased sales, decisive public relations activity at the right time gave an invaluable boost to Rentokil's image only a few months before the company went public.

Cutting Grass

The public cannot 'test drive' lawnmowers. Also three out of four are now sold off the shelf from supermarkets, cash and carries, etc, where the benefit of advice from experienced gardeners is not available.

It was against this background that the electric hover mowers from Flymo and Black & Decker had begun to capture a growing share of the popular mower market. These machines looked futuristic, and the public had been led to believe that only hover mowers could cut long and wet grass. Also, as the lower priced hovers had no grass collecting system—unlike the cylinder machines—it was even being suggested that leaving clippings uncollected was good for the lawn.

Not surprisingly, the light mains electric cylinder machine, the Qualcast Concorde, was being ignored by many potential purchasers.

Qualcast's consumer research confirmed this. But when consumers had the chance actually to try a hover and a Concorde side by side for themselves, most immediately changed their minds and much preferred the Concorde.

Ideally, Qualcast would have liked every potential purchaser of a light mains electric mower to try out, say, a hover and a Concorde side by side for themselves. As this was impossible, some other approach was needed.

Qualcast's public relations consultancy instead developed a campaign to invite the country's gardening writers to try out a Concorde and hover in their own gardens for up to two months during the summer.

All the gardening writers and broadcasters were sent an invitation to participate, along with a detailed match-mow test sheet designed to suggest certain points which the journalists might wish to compare.

67 journalists took part, from national and regional press, magazines, television and radio. Each was delivered a new Concorde and hover mower on a loan basis.

By the end of the year the results of the test sheets had been analysed. A massive majority of 49 journalists voted the Qualcast overall the better mower. Only six preferred the hover. Two felt the test came out equal and eight did not answer this question.

Equally important as the overall results were some of the detailed results on cutting power and handling, which demolished many of the hover myths along the way.

With the agreement of all the journalists involved, the results of the tests were published and 200,000 copies made available to dealers for use at point of sale. Extensive media coverage was generated about the campaign in the press, magazines, television and radio, giving valuable sales support.

The campaign was so successful that Qualcast subsequently used the results as the basis for a major colour press advertising campaign.

Sales of the Qualcast Concorde increased in volume by 24 per cent within six months and this imaginative public relations campaign was a successful component of the overall marketing mix in achieving the success.

Paint for the Community

Ask the man in the street what ICI stands for and he will probably conjure up words such as 'chemicals', 'technology' and 'innovation'.

Apply some of these words to a brand such as Dulux and you are probably going a long way towards describing an ideal brand image for a paint. But to round off that image it is necessary to create a reputation outside the strictly technological one.

Thus, when in the early 1960s the consumer marketeers at ICI Paints Division were reviewing strategy, they felt that the impact of the ICI roundel had to be complemented by a more 'human' face to the brand. After all, paint is to do with colour, fashion, fun and the home. Thus families began to appear in Dulux advertising and that famous English Sheepdog was 'born'.

In 1980, the Dulux Marketing Department decided that elements of its public relations programme should be aimed at adding further dimensions to the public's perception of the brand. In particular they wanted to link Dulux with a social/environmental activity but in a way that was *relevant* to their product. So sponsorship of a wildlife organisation would not do! From this brief the Dulux public relations consultancy, Welbeck, developed the Dulux Community Projects scheme. The basic concept was that Dulux would sponsor awards of paint to voluntary groups planning to carry out painting projects for the benefit of the community.

Any non-profit making organisation would be eligible to apply. The main criteria by which applications were to be judged were that the project should be creative, worthwhile and, most important, unlikely to take place unless a helping hand in the form of a paint donation was offered.

This latter point was particularly important, as Dulux had no desire to take sales away from its retail stockists—or work from professional decorators for that matter.

The scheme was launched in 1980 at a press conference held for home page and feature writers from national and local media, radio and TV. At the conference paint awards to a total retail value of £25,000 were announced.

The scheme was divided into two parts: an Initial Selection which would comprise all entries winning paint awards, and a Special Selection—those entries which were deemed by the judges to be the most interesting and, hence, worthy of additional cash awards. In Year One of the scheme some £2,000 was set aside for cash awards to be divided amongst the dozen or so best entries.

By 1984, the money allocated to paint awards had risen to £40,000 and the fund to cover the projects taking part in the Special Selection stood at £3,000.

Entries were encouraged by the publicity that resulted from the initial press conference and a direct mail campaign aimed at voluntary organisations.

As a result of the publicity and mailing, 7,000 leaflets and application forms were distributed in year one. From these 2,000 completed applications were returned.

In 1988, some 15,000 leaflets and application forms were distributed on request, resulting in some 5,000 completed applications; this number is increasing annually.

Many letters are received congratulating Dulux on the scheme, from successful and unsuccessful groups alike.

The launch of the Scheme each year is reported in national publications, on local radio and TV and in hundreds of local newspapers.

The greatest amount of coverage—almost 1,000 cuttings per year—is achieved in the local newspapers covering the paint-winning projects.

All the original objectives have been achieved in terms of entry numbers, letters received and media coverage. Now in its 8th year, the Dulux Community Projects Scheme has seen over 2,000 projects completed and over 120,000 enquiries dealt with by the Community Projects office at Welbeck. Some 250,000 litres of paint have been given away so far.

ICI Paints are more than satisfied that their principal objective of linking Dulux with a social/environmental activity relevant to their product is being achieved in a cost-effective fashion.

Using History—1 The Taj Mahal

'In 1631, the Emperor Shah Jahan of India commissioned the building of the exquisite jewel-like Taj Mahal to commemorate his wife, Empress Mumtaz Mahal. 350 years later, James Messenger has produced an exquisite jewel-like film, commemorating this "castle in the air, brought down to earth and fixed for the wonder of the ages" as the narrator says', wrote *Christian Science Monitor* commenting on the 28½-minute Taj Mahal film directed by James Messenger.

It all started in the autumn of 1980 when The Goodyear Tire & Rubber Company, Akron, Ohio, USA agreed to sponsor the film on the Taj Mahal, based on the script of James Messenger who, while on a visit to India, was fascinated by the enduring charm of this beautiful architectural masterpiece. His detailed proposal to Goodyear was based on the result of painstaking research in which he traced the contribution of the successive Mughal Emperors in bringing into India a new form of architecture, a synthesis of Persian and Indian style.

Goodyear saw the tremendous public relations opportunity of this film, as it was likely to attract a worldwide audience through the medium of television, cinema and private showings.

However, the Taj Mahal is no ordinary monument, and its filming posed many problems including obtaining permission from various Ministries. The Taj Mahal being the most treasured monument of India, there were several restrictions to its filming. Fortunately the Tourism Ministry recognised the vast potential of this film for projecting India abroad, and its importance as a vehicle of tourism promotion.

In Goodyear India's perspective, the Taj Mahal film could serve several public relations objectives. Firstly, the film would project Goodyear as closely involved in the promotion of Indian culture. Secondly, with its worldwide operations, Goodyear would be able to arrange exhibition of this film to a vast audience, which would develop an appreciation of India. Thirdly, through the sponsorship, Goodyear would contribute to more tourists visiting India. Fourthly, the exhibition of the film to private audiences through various business and social organisations would improve Goodyear's image among its customers. Lastly, the film project would bring Goodyear closer to many government officials, particularly the Ministries involved with the promotion of industry and tourism.

The project was carefully planned in detail before the film crew could arrive in India to begin shooting. Permission to shoot the film had to be processed through the Department of Archaeology, the Department of Tourism, and the External Affairs Ministry of the Government of India. The Ministry of Tourism and the Department of Archaeology went through the script, and carefully examined the authenticity of the facts presented.

With the help of the Ministry of Tourism, the shooting of the film was conducted with great speed. The first stage of the filming was scheduled in Delhi, which included filming at the Red Fort and Humayun's Tomb. The National Museum was kind enough to allow some paintings to be filmed. The Indian Tourism Development Corporation readily came forward with help to record some of the sound track of their Son et Lumière show at the Red Fort, in Delhi.

However, the actual filming at Agra was much more exciting. The crew spent over eight days filming various parts of the Taj Mahal. On occasion the filming continued almost non-stop for 18 hours. Jim Messenger and his team also spent time shooting the monuments of Agra Fort, Fatehpur Sikhri (the deserted city) and other Mughal Gardens and monuments. The second stage of the filming took place at the Mughal Garden of Kashmir.

The first Taj Mahal print arrived in India in December 1981. Prior to this, the film was shown to the Indian Ambassador in Washington and received his whole-hearted appreciation. In India, the management of Goodyear decided that before the film was shown to the public a special preview should be arranged for the Prime Minister, Mrs Gandhi.

The Prime Minister saw the film at her private residence with her family and the Information Advisor, H Y Sharda Prasad. The Public Relations Manager briefly explained the purpose behind Goodyear's sponsorship of the film. The Prime Minister approved the film and thanked Goodyear for their commendable effort.

Five weeks later, the film had its world première at the Convention Hall of the Ashoka Hotel, New Delhi, in the presence of Ministers,

Secretaries and Joint Secretaries of various Ministries, diplomats, industrialists, senior executives from private and public sector industries and prominent personalities from the field of art and culture.

A few weeks after the world première at New Delhi, the Taj Mahal film had its American première in Washington. Later, a special show was arranged at the White House for President and Mrs Reagan and other White House officials. The US Foreign Secretary, George Schultz, later visited India, and speaking to Indian newsmen, said that he was inspired by the film to visit India. His comments were reported in all leading newspapers in India.

On 30 July 1982, over 30 million Americans watched the Taj Mahal film on a nation-wide telecast over Public Broadcasting Service. During the Non-Aligned Meeting in New Delhi, it was the turn of Delhi television to telecast the film for the benefit of over 1,000 delegates, Government officials and Heads of the States visiting from 100 countries. Again at the time of the Commonwealth Prime Minister's Conference at New Delhi, the Taj Mahal film was telecast for the second time over Delhi Television.

Shortly after the Washington première, the Taj Mahal film won two awards in the United States. The Golden Eagle Award from CINE—the Council of International Non-Theatrical Events—in Washington, and the Silver Screen Award in the 1982 US Industrial Film Festival out of 1,000 entries from 21 countries.

Even today, many years after the film was inaugurated, The Taj Mahal film continues to draw private audiences at meetings, seminars, cocktail parties, club nights and other occasions.

Using History—2 The Navigators

Pacific Resources, Inc (PRI), a major energy company in Hawaii, has always strongly supported the preservation of Hawaiian culture and heritage. Historically it has sought ways—beyond its traditional energy-related activities—to make long-lasting, substantial contributions to the Pacific basin community it serves.

The opportunity arose in 1981 when remnants of an ancient Polynesian village, buried by a tidal wave more than 1,000 years ago, were discovered on Huahine in the Society Islands. Out of these ruins evolved a new and fascinating theory of the origin and culture of the ancient Polynesians.

PRI provided $25,000 to film the excavation work at this 'Polynesian Pompeii'. The footage subsequently became the basis for 'The Navigators', an hour-long documentary on an ancient seafaring people who were the first Polynesians. PRI was the film's major underwriter, providing funding of $191,000.

PRI had never undertaken a community relations project of this type before, so it conducted careful research to determine the impact of the proposed film and whether any similar project had ever been attempted.

PRI consulted with Public Broadcasting System's Hawaii affiliate, Hawaii Public Television, and learned no film of this kind had ever been produced locally or nationally. In addition, research showed that, although many other Hawaii companies also supported the preservation of Hawaii's culture and heritage, none had ever made a commitment of this kind before.

PRI also met with the community's education leaders, all of whom indicated a strong need for films, materials and projects which would help identify and perpetuate Hawaii's unique history and culture.

Responses from members of the community were especially positive, particularly since Hawaii would soon be celebrating its 25th anniversary of statehood, and public sentiment about rediscovering the Hawaiian people's heritage was high.

Finally, PRI considered the highly acclaimed and publicly supported Hokule'a experiment in 1976 in which a modern replica of an ancient Polynesian voyaging canoe sailed between Hawaii and Tahiti without the aid of navigational instruments. The voyage demonstrated both the seaworthiness of early Polynesian craft and the accuracy and sophistication of early Polynesian navigation. However, it was 'The Navigators' which would take this one step further, actually proving that the first Polynesians were skilled ocean voyagers from South East Asia who travelled vast distances across open waters to populate the remotest islands of the Pacific.

The primary objectives of 'The Navigators' film project were:

1   To recognise and honour the navigational accomplishments of the early Polynesians.

2   To build awareness and pride in the Polynesian people for their ancestors.

3   To provide an educational resource for future Polynesian generations on their heritage.

4   To position PRI as a company interested in enriching the community in which it operates.

Accomplishing these objectives, it was determined, would depend largely on public understanding of the reasons for producing the film; its educational value and historical significance; and public relations efforts to promote community interest in the project and support of the film.

PRI's initial intent was simply to provide funding for research and production of the film. However, to accomplish its objectives it became necessary for PRI also to undertake all promotional and marketing efforts.

An advisory committee was organised to provide direction and organisational support. It was comprised of PRI personnel; the film's producer; representatives from the company's public relations agencies; volunteers from Bishop Museum (whose archaeological crew unearthed the discovery at Huahine); and Hawaii Public Television.

Because of the complexity and long lead times needed for production and delivery of 'The Navigators' film, it was decided that the public relations effort would be conducted in two phases: Phase I would address the Huahine discovery and proposed film. Phase II would be a concentrated promotional effort for the film itself. Detailed public relations plans for both phases were developed for local and national implementation. PRI's challenge was to merge the two so that information presented to the public during Phase I would serve to generate community interest and support of the film during Phase II.

The Huahine discovery had a major social and historical impact on the Hawaii community. However, because it was two years before the resultant film was ready for broadcast, it was necessary to pursue other activities to preserve public interest and maintain momentum.

Press kits and support materials for both phases were developed. Speaking engagements and media interviews were scheduled, and feature stories placed in numerous local and national publications. A travelling photo exhibit on the film was created for public display, generating considerable community interest. Newsletters from various professional and community organisations followed the film's progress.

PRI also made 'The Navigators' a company-wide project, providing information and film updates, and asking for responses and suggestions from employees via the company's employee publications and in-house video programme.

Because PRI felt the educational value of 'The Navigators' should be emphasised, educational supplements that could be incorporated into a school's curriculum were produced and distributed to Hawaii's schools.

As activities escalated, publicity also increased dramatically. The publicity generated an outpouring of community interest and support and prompted the Arthur Vining Davis Foundations and Hawaii Committee for the Humanities to provide additional grants for development of support materials.

To celebrate the film's completion, PRI hosted a gala film première attended by more than 500 prominent leaders in business, industry, government, and the culture and the arts community. Media attendance was high, and there was major print and broadcast coverage as well as editorial endorsements for 'The Navigators', both preceding and following the film première.

And, validating its contribution to the film industry, 'The Navigators' was accepted by PBS for prime-time airing on more than 300 public stations across the United States in October 1983.

The results of 'The Navigators' were immediate, measurable and gratifying. Community reaction to the film was positive, and national Nielsen ratings were high. Results of the ratings showed more than three million people in Hawaii and across the nation watched 'The Navigators'. It was rebroadcast nationally on 8 September 1984.

In addition, the East West Research Institute conducted a survey of Hawaii residents to assess public awareness and attitudes towards the film. The survey indicated in a sample of 600 people that 39 per cent, or 234 people, had either seen or read about 'The Navigators'. Of those who saw the film in Hawaii, 80 per cent rated it favourably, and 78 per cent identified PRI as the sponsor.

'The Navigators' proved to be much more than an entertaining film or educational tool. It became a living history, the missing chapter in the story of the first Polynesians and their settlement of the vast Pacific.

Gimmicks and Off-beat Public Relations

Gimmicks in public relations are justified only when there is a serious objective to be achieved. The supporting of a London double-decker bus on four Wedgwood china teacups was an excellent example of the successful public relations use of the gimmick, drawing attention to the remarkable strength of china despite the common belief that it is fragile.

The event took place near the Tower of London and the photographs used widely in the press showed Tower Bridge in the background thus adding a sense of authenticity.

A new expression for this type of programme is 'creative public relations' and some consultancies have appointed creative directors. This is a rather strange development as public relations should always be pro-active as well as reactive.

There is plenty of scope for dreaming up unusual situations which will attract public attention but it is essential to use these gimmicks with discretion. As in all aspects of public relations, care in planning and timing is the key to success and it is always necessary to ensure that these 'creative' ideas and situations do not cause obstruction or embarrass members of the public.

17 Entering Public Relations

The preceding chapters have shown that public relations is not an exact science. To be a successful public relations practitioner demands a wide range of qualities and skills. The man or woman who aspires to reach the top rank needs to have sound judgment, personal integrity, a specialist knowledge of methods of communication, organising ability of a high standard, management skills, and above all a strong personality and a capacity for leadership.

There is not room at the top for everybody, of course, and many people may prefer to specialise in a particular branch of the work, such as investor relations, public affairs, media relations or exhibitions. It is very helpful, however, to have had experience in all branches of public relations before deciding to specialise. This is because no public relations function stands alone, and even in large departments where the work is sectionalised it is most useful to be able to double up in case of overload, sickness or other emergency.

EDUCATIONAL REQUIREMENTS
In the past, men and women have entered the field of public relations with all types of academic backgrounds. Entry has been related more to an individual's communications skills than to his or her background. Recruitment, however, has concentrated on those with journalism degrees, since writing skill is of major importance and because organisations have first recognised their public relations

needs in the areas of media relations and publication production.

Journalism schools in the USA have responded by adding public relations courses; today, one hundred colleges and universities in the United States provide bachelor and graduate programmes of study in public relations. The number of US educational institutions with accredited programmes also continues to increase.

Many of these programmes are oriented toward media relations, whereas a communications management orientation is needed in which the student is thoroughly educated in the social sciences and management and familiarised with a broad range of communications knowledge.

Faculty members are needed in public relations with interdisciplinary backgrounds in anthropology, sociology, psychology, political science, management, and law as well as communications so that students will benefit from the diversity of approach to communications management. The diversity of academic backgrounds would also greatly benefit the profession by encouraging interdisciplinary approaches to public relations' research needs. (See the 'Wheel of Education' on page 21).

In the United Kingdom, the first university degree course in public relations, an MSc, one year full time, was introduced in the University of Stirling in September 1988. In September 1989, BA(Hons) degrees in public relations are offered at two colleges of higher education, one at Plymouth and the other at Poole. These are likely to be followed by other bachelor degree courses. The University of Stirling has announced the introduction of an MSc in public relations by distance learning.

Mature students are welcome at all these new degree courses in Britain.

Students interested in public relations should keep in mind that a strong base is needed in the social sciences to understand how man communicates, adapts to change, behaves within small groups, organisations, and social structures. An understanding of man's needs, how he is motivated and persuaded, how he adapts to change, and how he functions best is also important.

In addition, the student needs to understand political systems and government and management theory.

Skill development is needed in writing, editing, speech, and graphic design in particular, with as much exposure as possible to the full range of communications techniques provided by today's technology.

The student also needs to acquaint himself or herself with the terminology of the business world through course work in business and with the terminology of the scientific community through the acquisition of course work in the basic sciences. The 'working' language needed, however, will depend upon the field of public relations the student wishes to enter. Public relations students interested in the entertainment field, for example, will find familiarity with the arts or sports more important than knowledge in other areas.

Academic training is by no means an assurance of a successful career in public relations, which demands qualities not easily measurable in examinations. The following list details some of these necessary qualities.

1 Abundant common sense.

2 First-class organising ability.

3 Good judgment, objectivity, and keen critical ability.

4 Imagination and the ability to appreciate the other person's point of view.

5 Imperturbability.

6 An infinite capacity for detail.

7 A lively inquisitive mind.

8 Willingness to work long and unsocial hours when necessary.

9 Resilience and a sense of humour.

10 Flexibility and the ability to deal with many different problems at the same time.

In addition to these qualities, it is essential to possess the ability to write well, and to be capable of correcting and copyreading other people's writing. The need for a positive personality has been mentioned and it is desirable that this should be supported by a pleasant voice and the ability for public speaking and persuasive presentation.

TRAINING COURSES

Hundreds of short training courses are available to those wishing to improve their public relations skills. Most are offered by public relations organisations but universities and colleges are also offering courses.

There are a number of diploma and degree courses in Britain and other countries on various aspects of communication and media studies, film and media. These courses overlap to a certain degree with public relations but do not provide the professional experience element which is so important.

Many colleges of further education and polytechnics in Britain teach the Communication, Advertising and Marketing Education Foundation (CAM) Certificate and Diploma syllabuses, both of which include public relations. These CAM courses are usually taken part-time while working in the profession. Details are available from CAM, Abford House, 15 Wilton Road, London SW1V 1NJ.

In the past it was argued that practical experience as a journalist was a most desirable attribute in anyone wishing to enter public relations. This may be true of those who wish to make a career in media relations, but since so much of the work lies outside the press field there is no logical reason why a journalist should necessarily make a good public relations practitioner. Journalism does, however, develop certain habits of thought and actions such as objectivity, resourcefulness, and breadth of vision, which are valuable in public relations. A thorough working knowledge of the press is essential to those engaged in public relations, but it is possible to acquire this without having actually worked on a newspaper.

A CAREER FOR WOMEN

Public relations is one of the careers that offer equal opportunities to women. Some of the women in public relations work for organisations or in fields that are characteristically feminine, such as the fashion or the food industries, but many others work for heavy industry. In many instances they are heads of public relations departments, and there is no reason why women should remain in subordinate positions in public relations when they have the ability and desire to reach the top.

In a number of instances in the past, young women wishing to enter public relations have trained as shorthand-typist/secretaries and have joined public relations companies or departments to do secretarial work. This method of obtaining a foothold in public relations had some merit in the past when there were few opportunities of obtaining practical experience, but it is not to be recommended today except in cases where a young woman feels she would like to observe public relations from the inside before deciding to make it her career.

Five 'Deadly Sins'

A careful study of this book should have given a clear impression of the 'do's and don'ts' of public relations, but a fitting conclusion to this chapter may be a list of the 'deadly sins' to be avoided by all those who wish to make a successful career in public relations:

1   Never speak about public relations in highfaluting mumbo-jumbo.

2   Do not seek personal publicity.

3   Never apologise for the views of the chairman or other chief executives.

4   Never patronise or talk down to the media.

5   Never think of, or speak of, media relations as being synonymous with public relations. Similarly, do not accept the view that public relations is a part of marketing.

Avoid the use of the initials PR as they are misleading and ambiguous. It is quite possible to avoid using the initials PR and PRO as evidenced by the fact that they have not been used by the author in this book. The initials are all too often used in a derogatory context.

18 How it all began

Public relations has been practised sporadically since the earliest times even though the name is of comparatively recent origin. Before discussing the modern history, it is interesting to recall some early examples of public relations activities in different parts of the world.

From Greek and Roman Times to 1914
There is ample evidence in the records of the early Greek and Roman empires to show that great care and attention was devoted to the influencing of public opinion. Public relations in those far-off days appears to have been an integral part of government. The Romans dramatised the importance of public opinion in the slogan *vox populi, vox dei*—the voice of the people is the voice of God.

In more recent history, the American Revolution was started by a small group of men, including Samuel Adams, Thomas Paine, Benjamin Franklin, Alexander Hamilton and Thomas Jefferson, who used voice and pen to make a profound effect on the public opinion of their day. They circulated pamphlets, wrote in the press, lectured and spread their ideas of revolt by word of mouth.

In England, the pamphleteers of the eighteenth century, men such as Jonathan Swift and Daniel Defoe, were using methods to propagate their ideas that had much in common with present-day public relations practice. This applies also to the work of Huxley to promote the evolutionary ideas of Darwin, and the writings of Charles Dickens to expose the social evils of his time.

There is no need to multiply examples to prove the point that public relations practice is nearly as old as the world itself. All that is new is the proliferation of the idea consequent on the industrialisation and intensification of modern life and the availability of the new means of communication. The former has created the need for public relations, the new mass media have provided the tools.

Development in the United States
The first actual use of the phrase 'public relations' is thought to have been in 1807 when President Thomas Jefferson, drafting his 'Seventh Address to Congress' in his own hand, scratched out the words 'state of thought' in one place and wrote in 'public relations' instead.

That colourful personality, Ivy L Lee, left a poorly-paid job as a reporter in 1903 and started as a press agent. His work as personal adviser to John D Rockefeller, Jr, began in December 1914, but it was not until 1919 that he began to use the term 'public relations'. Lee contributed many of the techniques and principles that characterise public relations today, and he was among the first to realise the fallacy of publicity unsupported by good works. His success in altering the public image of John D Rockefeller, Sr, from a 'greedy old capitalist' to a kindly old man who gave dimes to children and millions of dollars to charity, has become a legend. See also Chapter 3 for further information about Ivy Lee.

The First World War gave public relations a big impetus in the USA. President Wilson set up the Committee on Public Information in response to a suggestion by a journalist friend, George Creel. The Creel Committee grew into a vast enterprise which demonstrated the power of organised publicity.

Among many talented men and women working for the Creel Committee was Edward L Bernays, a nephew of Sigmund Freud. Bernays coined the term 'public relations counsel', and his book *Crystallising Public Opinion,* published in 1923, was the first full-length book dealing with public relations.

Between the wars there was a remarkable expansion of public relations activities in every walk of American life. The advent of the Second World War accelerated this tendency, and once again the Government led the way with the formation of the Office of War

Information under Elmer Davis. The OWI encouraged extensive expansion of public relations in the armed forces, in industry, and in allied fields. Many of today's leading practitioners served their apprenticeship in the gigantic public relations programme which dwarfed the efforts of the earlier Creel Committee.

United States presidents have had a major role in improving public understanding of the importance of public relations activity. President Andrew Jackson was the first to rely heavily on journalists for advice and staff assistance. President Franklin Delano Roosevelt used the radio for his famous fireside chats in order to build confidence and achieve support for his programmes. The approach was used later by President John F Kennedy with the new communication medium, television.

Public relations, although still misunderstood as a function by many in the United States, has grown rapidly as a professional area. The Public Relations Society of America, The International Association of Business Communicators, state public relations associations, and specialised public relations associations have increased their memberships one hundred per cent or more during the past decade.

The growth of academic programmes in public relations in colleges and universities throughout the United States and a growing student interest in public relations and the job opportunities that continue to develop for graduates has brought public relations in the US to the point of professional recognition.

Development in the UK

In Britain the first stirrings of organised public relations were probably the efforts made by the Insurance Commission in 1911, under the instructions of Lloyd George, to explain the National Insurance Act. The outbreak of war in 1914 led to a rapid expansion of official publicity in Britain and overseas, which was at first carried out by a number of separate bodies. By early in 1918 such publicity was conducted in the main by three organisations: the Ministry of Information, responsible for publicity work in the Dominions and in Allied and neutral countries; the National War Aims Committee, which carried out patriotic propaganda in Britain; and a committee, under Lord Northcliffe, which was responsible for propaganda in enemy countries. It might be fair to describe this work as a mixture of public relations and propaganda.

These organisations were abolished after the war, but some of their functions were transformed to other departments, principally to the News Department of the Foreign Office. The Air Ministry had a press officer from its inception in 1919, and in the same year the Ministry of Health set up a Housing Information Department. In 1920 the British Library of Information (the forerunner of the present-day British Information Services) was established in New York, and at about the same time press attachés were appointed to the British embassies in Paris, Rome and Berlin. In 1932 a Chief Press Liaison Officer was appointed to the Prime Minister's staff.

Press relations was thus becoming accepted in Government circles. In 1918 the post of Press Secretary to the King was established.

In 1926 the establishment of the Empire Marketing Board marked the first use of public relations as we understand it today. The late Sir Stephen Tallents, founder president of the Institute of Public Relations, was selected to run the new venture which had as its object 'bringing the Empire alive to the mind of people in Britain'. the EMB used films, posters, exhibitions, the press and the BBC to publicise its objectives. About one-third of its annual grant of £1,000,000 from the Government was spent on publicity.

The work of the Empire Marketing Board was cut short by the onset of the serious economic crisis in the autumn of 1931. At short notice, the EMB was ordered to switch all its resources to the launching of a full-scale campaign in support of the Prime Minister's appeal to 'Buy British'. All media of communication were employed, and the campaign received widespread support. Its success surpassed expectations and proved—for the first time in Britain—the benefits that can come from a well-conceived and energetically administered public relations campaign.

Sir Stephen Tallents continued his policy of using the best available artists, film makers and other experts when he became Public Relations Officer to the Post Office in 1933. This appointment is thought by many to have been the first use of the term in the United Kingdom, having been taken by the Postmaster-General, the late Sir Kingsley Wood, from American practice.

There were also important developments during the 1930s in the field of overseas information. The BBC established its Empire Service in 1932, the basis on which the BBC External Broadcasting

Services were subsequently built up. Then in 1934 the British Council came into being to foster educational and cultural relations with overseas countries.

The general pattern of development was the establishment of press offices to deal with inquiries, developing into public relations divisions. By 1939 there were public relations departments in nearly all the social service departments (such as the Ministry of Labour and the Ministry of Health) and in the three departments dealing with the armed forces.

The Ministry of Information, 1939-46

At the outbreak of war in 1939 a Ministry of Information was again set up. This large-scale government public relations project was paralleled by the setting up of public relations units in all branches of the armed forces. The MOI made a massive contribution to the successful prosecution of the war, and the team of all talents produced some remarkably effective results. When the war ended it was decided to replace the MOI by a non-ministerial department—the Central Office of Information—which has been described fully in Chapter 14.

Public Relations in Local Government and Industry

The appointment of a public relations officer by the National Association of Local Government Officers (now known as the National and Local Government Officers' Association) in 1937 was supplemented by a system of honorary district and branch public relations officers. The progress of public relations in local government was discussed in Chapter 15.

British industry did not show very much interest in public relations until 1945, but since then the increase in industrial public relations in the United Kingdom has been rapid. The chapters dealing with the various media, and the chapter dealing with finance and industry (Chapter 13), have described the lines on which public relations has developed in industry during the last 50 years.

In general, it is noteworthy that whilst public relations in the business sphere started and blossomed in the USA, the development of public relations in governmental, political and non-commercial fields has been pioneered in Britain.

The IPR and the PRCA

The Institute of Public Relations was formed in the UK in February 1948 and has played a significant part in the development of the profession. The Public Relations Consultants Association (PRCA) is the trade association of public relations consultancies and has been very active in regularising consultancy.

The formation of the International Public Relations Association (IPRA) is described in Appendix II.

Public Relations World-wide

Since 1948 the development of public relations has been rapid in most countries, both North and South, but at varying rates.

In Latin America there has been a very positive advance due to the active programme of the Inter-American Confederation of Public Relations Associations (FIARP).

Countries which have shown considerable initiative in promoting public relations practice and where there are active national public relations associations include: Argentina, Australia, Austria, Bangladesh, Belgium, Brazil, Canada, Denmark, Egypt, Finland, France, Germany, Ghana, Greece, Hong Kong, India, Indonesia, Ireland, Israel, Italy, Japan, Kenya, Korea, Malaysia, The Netherlands, Nigeria, Norway, The Philippines, Singapore, South Africa, Spain, Sweden, Switzerland, Thailand, Trinidad and Tobago, Turkey and Zimbabwe.

Public relations practice is now recognised in many other countries and IPRA now has members in Bulgaria, China, Cyprus, Hungary, Kuwait, Mauritius, Netherland Antilles, Oman, Poland, Saudi Arabia, Sudan, Uganda, USSR and Zambia.

19 International Public Relations and the Interdependent World

The growth of global communication by satellite has brought the idea of the interdependent world into an everyday reality. Television screens bring immediate pictures of political events and natural disasters from all over the world.

Many important factors have increased interdependence. They include new developments in science and technology, especially computers and the growing sophistication of software. Fibre optics, electronic mail and telefax transmission have all speeded up communication but differences in values, beliefs and laws persist. A public relations programme which may be ideal for North America is likely to be less successful in Britain and may be quite inappropriate for other countries.

The essential principle in international public relations must always be 'Think globally but act locally'.

The Worlds of Public Relations

There are two separate worlds of public relations. One consists of all the practitioners world-wide who practise public relations for the benefit of their employers and clients. The other world is the very wide range of activities which falls within the limits of public relations practice. Page 2 lists ten different fields in which public relations can make a significant contribution and thirteen different avenues in which practitioners work.

The theory and philosophy of public relations practice is very similar in most countries but the performance can be very different as it depends so much on economic factors, business customs, language, culture and religion.

It is very fortunate if one can communicate with all ones publics and audiences in one language and can assume a satisfactory level of literacy. This still applies in Britain to a large extent but many countries have to communicate in two or more official languages plus important local dialects. Illiteracy is still a problem even in some industrial countries. These factors emphasise the need for public relations and media programmes to be tailored to the requirements of local conditions.

It is therefore necessary to identify objectives precisely in international public relations if successful results and cost effectiveness are to be achieved. Working in a local environment, any publicity which is truthful is likely to have beneficial results, but if the objectives are international it is essential to pinpoint targets and objectives.

Most of the methods used in international public relations are the same as used in any other aspect of the profession and have been described earlier in this book.

Problems of translation and interpreting were discussed in Chapter 12, pages 150-151, under the heading 'Speaking in the Right Language' and the following paragraph mentioned the pitfalls of 'Body Language'. Public relations can be very supportive of exporting as described on pages 148-150 and the chapter on 'Exhibitions' is also most relevant.

Methods of organising public relations in a multinational or a large company with overseas subsidiaries have been dealt with on pages 142-143 and the advantages of working with others sharing common interests were emphasised.

Analysing Trends
The Mexican Statement (see page 4) stresses the importance of analysing trends and predicting their consequences. This is sometimes called 'environmental scanning' or 'operational research' and is particularly important in the international field. All multinationals pay close attention to issues and trends likely to affect future prospects and public relations practitioners are eminently qualified to play a constructive part in this 'crystal gazing'.

Networking

Networking deserves some comment. If public relations advice or services are required in a number of different countries, it is very difficult, if not impossible, to run it successfully from headquarters. Local know-how is essential as explained above.

A large company may set up its own public relations departments attached to each main overseas subsidiary. It is more likely that the chosen solution will be to employ public relations consultancies in the main territories.

The largest consultancies have branch offices in many countries and one choice is to engage one of these agencies who offer a 'local' service but controlled from headquarters. Another option is to use public relations consultants who belong to an international network of small and medium size consultancies which work together as required. Here there is a choice between a number of networks, some of them financially integrated, while others remain quite independent but work together as required to serve their clients' needs.

Most consultancies which operate internationally have their senior members in the International Public Relations Association which is a reliable source of information on this aspect of public relations. (See Appendix II).

All public relations practitioners doing work of international significance are likely to be members of IPRA, both those working in-house and for consultancies. The growth of IPRA has coincided with the rapid development of international public relations. The establishment of high levels of performance and professional standards owes much to the influence of IPRA and the regular world congresses, meetings and seminars which it organises world-wide. These bring together senior men and women working in public relations and have helped to develop the two 'worlds' referred to earlier in this chapter.

Public relations knows no frontiers and the advent of perestroika and glasnost will do much to make the acceptance and efficient use of public relations really international. 'Think globally but always act locally'.

Appendix I

Codes of Professional Conduct and Ethics

The following code of conduct was adopted by the International Public Relations Association at its general assembly in Venice, May 1961 and is binding on all members of the Association.

IPRA CODE OF PROFESSIONAL CONDUCT

A *Personal and Professional Integrity*

1 It is understood that by personal integrity is meant the maintenance of both high moral standards and a sound reputation. By professional integrity is meant observance of the Constitution, rules and, particularly, the Code as adopted by IPRA.

B *Conduct towards Clients and Employers*

1 A member has a general duty of fair dealing towards his clients or employers, past and present.

2 A member shall not represent conflicting or competing interests without the express consent of those concerned.

3 A member shall safeguard the confidences of both present and former clients or employers.

4 A member shall not employ methods tending to be derogatory of another member's client or employer.

5 In performing services for a client or employer a member shall not accept fees, commissions or any other valuable consideration in connection with those services from anyone other than his client or employer without the express consent of his client or employer, given after a full disclosure of the facts.

6   A member shall not propose to a prospective client or employer that his fee or other compensation be contingent on the achievement of certain results; nor shall he enter into any fee agreement to the same effect.

C   *Conduct towards the Public and the Media*

1   A member shall conduct his professional activities in accordance with the public interest, and with full respect for the dignity of the individual.

 2   A member shall not engage in any practice which tends to corrupt the integrity of channels of public communication.

3   A member shall not intentionally disseminate false or misleading information.

4   A member shall at all times seek to give a balanced and faithful representation of the organisation which he serves.

5   A member shall not create any organisation to serve some announced cause but actually to serve an undisclosed special or private interest of a member or his client or his employer, nor shall he make use of it or any such existing organisation.

D   *Conduct towards Colleagues*

1   A member shall not intentionally injure the professional reputation or practice of another member. However, if a member has evidence that another member has been guilty of unethical, illegal or unfair practices in violation of this Code, he should present the information to the Council of IPRA.

2   A member shall not seek to supplant another member with his employer or client.

3   A member shall cooperate with fellow members in upholding and enforcing this Code.

CODE OF ATHENS

IPRA members are also required to abide by a code of ethics, known as the Code of Athens as it was adopted in Athens in May 1965 by the IPRA General Assembly. It was modified slightly in Tehran in April 1968. (The Code of Athens was also adopted by CERP in 1965).

This code obliges every IPRA member to observe a strict moral code. Each member:

Shall endeavour

1   To contribute to the achievement of the moral and cultural conditions enabling human beings to reach their full stature and enjoy the indefeasible rights to which they are entitled under the 'Universal Declaration of Human Rights'.

2   To establish communications patterns and channels which, fostering the free flow of essential information, will make each member of the society in

which he lives feel that he is being kept informed, and also give him an awareness of his own personal involvement and responsibility, and of his solidarity with other members.

3 To bear in mind that, because of the relationship between his profession and the public, his conduct—even in private—will have an impact on the way in which the profession as a whole is appraised.

4 To respect, in the course of his professional duties, the moral principles and rules of the 'Universal Declaration of Human Rights'.

5 To pay due regard to, and uphold, human dignity, and to recognise the right of each individual to judge for himself.

6 To encourage the moral, psychological and intellectual conditions for dialogue in its true sense, and to recognise the right of these parties involved to state their case and express their views.

Shall undertake

7 To conduct himself always and in all circumstances in such a manner as to deserve and secure the confidence of those with whom he comes into contact.

8 To act, in all circumstances, in such a manner as to take account of the respective interests of the parties involved: both the interests of the organisation which he serves and the interests of the publics concerned.

9 To carry out his duties with integrity, avoiding language likely to lead to ambiguity or misunderstanding, and to maintain loyalty to his clients or employers, whether past or present.

Shall refrain from

10 Subordinating the truth to other requirements.

11 Circulating information which is not based on established and ascertainable facts.

12 Taking part in any venture or undertaking which is unethical or dishonest or capable of impairing human dignity and integrity.

13 Using any 'manipulative' methods or techniques designed to create subconscious motivations which the individual cannot control of his own free will and so cannot be held accountable for the action taken on them.

Most national public relations associations have adopted codes of professional conduct which must be observed by their members. The Code of Professional Conduct of the Institute of Public Relations, which was adopted on 31 December 1963, is typical of these codes.

IPR CODE OF PROFESSIONAL CONDUCT

The essential disciplines of good public behaviour by individuals and organisations are set out in The Institute of Public Relations Code of Professional Conduct. Additionally the Public Relations Consultants

Association has a Code of Consultancy Practice which applies to its member consultancies.

As with other professional bodies accustomed to observing ethical standards, the fact that a public relations practitioner or organisation undertakes to conform with certain ground rules is an assurance of reputable business dealing.

It should be emphasised that IPR members undertake to observe the Institute's Code when applying to join. It is recommended that they should draw the attention of clients and employers to the Code whenever appropriate.

Members should also make themselves aware of the Codes adopted by International groupings within the public relations profession, particularly the Codes of Athens and Lisbon which the IPR supports.

The IPR Code of Professional Practice was reviewed in 1985 and revisions adopted by special resolution at the Institute's annual general meeting on 9 April 1986.

1 *Standards of Professional Conduct.* A member shall have a positive duty to observe the highest standards in the practice of public relations. Furthermore a member has the personal responsibility at all times to deal fairly and honestly with his client, employer and employees, past or present, with fellow members, with the media of communication and above all else with the public.

2 *Media of communication.* A member shall not engage in any practice which tends to corrupt the integrity of the media of communication.

3 *Undisclosed interests.* A member shall have the duty to ensure that the actual interest of any organisation with which he may be professionally concerned is adequately declared.

4 *Rewards to holders of public office.* A member shall not, with intent to further his interests (or those of his client or employer), offer to give any reward to a person holding public office if such action is inconsistent with the public interest.

5 *Dissemination of information.* A member shall have a positive duty at all times to respect the truth and in this regard not to disseminate false or misleading information knowingly or recklessly and to use proper care to avoid doing so inadvertently.

6 *Confidential information.* A member shall not disclose (except upon the order of a court of competent jurisdiction) or make use of information given or obtained in confidence from his employer or client, past or present, for personal gain or otherwise.

7 *Conflict of interests.* A member shall not represent conflicting interests but may represent competing interests with the express consent of the parties concerned.

8 *Disclosure of beneficial financial interests.* A member with a beneficial financial interest in or from an organisation shall not recommend the use of

that organisation, nor make use of its services on behalf of his client or employer, without declaring his interest.

9 *Payment contingent upon achievements.* A member shall not negotiate or agree terms with a prospective employer or client on the basis of payment contingent upon specific future public relations achievements.

10 *Employment of holders of public office.* A member who employs or is responsible for employing or recruiting a member of either House of Parliament, a member of the European Parliament or a person elected to public office, whether in a consultative or executive capacity, shall disclose this fact, also the object and nature of the employment to the Executive Director of the Institute who shall enter it in a register kept for the purpose. A member of the Institute who himself falls into any of these categories shall be directly responsible for disclosing or causing to be disclosed to the Executive Director the same information as may relate to himself. (The register referred to in this clause shall be open to public inspection at the offices of the Institute during office hours).

11 *Injury to other members.* A member shall not maliciously injure the professional reputation of another member.

12 *Reputation of the profession.* A member shall not conduct himself in a manner which is or is likely to be detrimental to the reputation of the Institute or the profession of public relations.

13 *Upholding the code.* A member shall uphold this Code, shall cooperate with fellow members in so doing and in enforcing decisions on any matter arising from its application. If a member has reason to believe that another member has been engaged in practices which may be in breach of this Code, it shall be his duty first to inform the member concerned and then to inform the Institute if these practices do not cease. It is the duty of all members to assist the Institute to implement this Code, and the Institute will support any member so doing.

14 *Other professions.* A member shall, when working in association with other professionals, respect the codes of other professions and shall not knowingly be party to any breach of such codes.

15 *Professional updating.* A member shall be expected to be aware of, understand and observe this Code, any amendments to it and any other codes which shall be incorporated into this Code and to remain uptodate with the content and recommendations of any guidance or practice papers as may be issued by the Institute and shall have a duty to take all reasonable steps to conform to good practice as expressed in such guidance or practice papers.

16 *Instruction of others.* A member shall not knowingly cause or permit another person or organisation to act in a manner inconsistent with this Code or be a party to such action.

The IPR issues an Interpretation of this Code which can be obtained from the IPR at Gate House, 1 St John's Square, London EC1M 4DH.

EUROPEAN CODE OF PROFESSIONAL CONDUCT IN PUBLIC RELATIONS (Code of Lisbon)

This code was approved by the General Assembly of the European Confederation of Public Relations (CERP) at Lisbon on 16 April 1978 and amended on 13 May 1989. Nearly all the European public relations associations are members of CERP so this code is binding on all their members.

SECTION I *Criteria and standards of professional qualification of practitioners bound by this Code.*

Clause 1
Every professional member of (national association) duly admitted as such in accordance with the rules of (national association) is deemed for the purpose of this Code to be a public relations practitioner, and to be bound by the Code.

SECTION II *General professional obligations.*

Clause 2
In the practice of his profession, the public relations practitioner undertakes to respect the principles set forth in the Universal Declaration of Human Rights, and in particular the freedom of expression and the freedom of the press which give effect to the right of the individual to receive information.

He likewise undertakes to act in accordance with the public interest and not to harm the dignity or integrity of the individual.

Clause 3
In his professional conduct, the public relations practitioner must show honesty, intellectual integrity, and loyalty. In particular he undertakes not to make use of comment or information which, to his knowledge or belief, are false or misleading. In the same spirit he must be careful to avoid the use, even by accident, of practices or methods incompatible with this Code.

Clause 4
Public relations activities must be carried out openly; they must be readily identifiable, bear a clear indication of their origin, and must not tend to mislead third parties.

Clause 5
In his relations with other professions and with other branches of social communications, the public relations practitioner must respect the rules and practices appropriate to those professions or occupations, so far as these are compatible with the ethics of his own profession.

A public relations practitioner must respect the national code of professional conduct and the laws in force in any country in which he practises his profession and exercise restraint in seeking personal publicity.

Section III   *Specific professional obligations.*

● *TOWARDS CLIENTS OR EMPLOYERS*

Clause 6
A public relations practitioner shall not represent conflicting or competing interests without the express consent of the clients or employers concerned.

Clause 7
In the practice of his profession, a public relations practitioner must observe complete discretion. He must scrupulously respect professional confidence, and in particular must not reveal any confidential information received from his clients or employers, past, present or potential, or make use of such information, without express authorisation.

Clause 8
A public relations practitioner who has an interest which may conflict with that of his client or employer must disclose it as soon as possible.

Clause 9
A public relations practitioner must not recommend to his client or employer the services of any business or organisation in which he has a financial, commercial or other interest without first disclosing that interest.

Clause 10
A public relations practitioner shall not enter a contract with his client or employer under which the practitioner guarantees quantified results.

Clause 11
A public relations practitioner may accept remuneration for his services only in the form of salary or fees, and on no account may he accept payment or other material rewards contingent upon quantifiable professional results.

Clause 12
A public relations practitioner shall not accept for his services to a client or an employer any remuneration from a third party, such as discounts, commissions or payments in kind, except with the agreement of the client or employer.

Clause 13
When the execution of a public relations assignment would be likely to entail serious professional misconduct and imply behaviour contrary to the principles of this Code, the public relations practitioner must take steps to notify his client or employer immediately, and do everything possible to see that the latter respects the requirements of the Code. If the client or employer persists in his intentions, the practitioner must nevertheless observe the Code irrespective of the consequences to him.

● *TOWARDS PUBLIC OPINION AND THE INFORMATION MEDIA*

Clause 14

The spirit of this Code and the rules contained in preceding clauses, notably clauses 2, 3, 4 and 5, imply a constant concern on the part of the public relations practitioner with the right to information, and moreover the duty to provide information, within the limits of professional confidence. They imply also a respect for the rights and independence of the information media.

Clause 15

Any attempt to deceive public opinion or its representatives is forbidden.

News must be provided without charge or hidden reward for its use or publication.

Clause 16

If it should seem necessary to maintain the initiative in, and the control of, the distribution of information, within the principles of this Code, the public relations practitioner may buy space or broadcasting time in conformity with the rules, practices and usages in that field.

● *TOWARDS FELLOW-PRACTITIONERS*

Clause 17

The public relations practitioner must refrain from unfair competition with fellow practitioners.

He must neither act nor speak in a way which would tend to depreciate the reputation or business of a fellow practitioner, subject always to his duty under Clause 19b of this Code.

● *TOWARDS THE PROFESSION*

Clause 18

The public relations practitioner must refrain from any conduct which may prejudice the reputation of his profession.

In particular he must not cause harm to his national association (name), its efficient working, or its good name, by malicious attacks or by any breach of its constitution or rules.

Clause 19

The reputation of the profession is the responsibility of each of its members. The public relations practitioner has a duty not only to respect this Code himself but also:

a) to assist in making the Code more widely and better known and understood;

b) to report to the competent disciplinary authorities any breach or suspected breach of the Code which comes to his notice, and

c) to take any action in his power to ensure that rulings on its application by such authorities are observed and sanctions made effective.

Any practitioner who permits a violation of the Code will be considered as having himself breached the Code.

Appendix II

International Public Relations Association (IPRA)

The concept of an international public relations association came into being in November 1949 when two Dutch and four British public relations men met in London. As they talked of their work they developed the idea of organising public relations people into a para-national society, the objective of which would be to raise the standard of public relations practice in the various countries, and improve the professional quality and efficiency of public relations practitioners.

As an outcome of this informal talk in London, a group of public relations executives from Britain, the Netherlands, France, Norway and the United States of America met in Holland in March 1950 under the auspices of the Royal Netherlands International Trade Fair and the Public Relations Society of Holland.

After full discussion, these pioneers issued a statement that having considered the necessity of furthering the skill and ethics of their profession, and of a clearer understanding of their work, and having considered further the value of international exchange of information and cooperation they resolved that a Provisional International Committee be set up with the object of promoting such exchange and cooperation and the eventual establishment of an International Public Relations Association.

A Provisional International Committee was formed and during the next five years regular meetings were held in England—usually in conjunction with the annual Weekend Conference of the Institute of Public Relations. These meetings were attended by representatives from France, Great Britain, the Netherlands, Norway and the United States of America with, on some occasions, observers from Australia, Belgium, Canada, Finland, Italy and Switzerland.

The International Public Relations Association (IPRA) was established in London on 1 May 1955. A Constitution was formally adopted, and the first IPRA Council was appointed.

IPRA is now a world-wide professional and fraternal organisation which serves as a catalyst in the continuing development of the highest possible standards of public relations education, ethics, practice and performance.

Through its regular meetings in different parts of the world and its publications, platforms are provided for furthering knowledge and understanding of different professional techniques and styles.

At each triennial public relations world congress, IPRA publishes a 'Gold Paper' on a current topic. Gold Paper No 6 'Public Relations and Propaganda—values compared' was published in April 1988 and previous gold papers dealt with 'The Communicative Society', education and research.

In 1961 IPRA adopted its formal 'Code of Conduct' as the required guidelines of practice for all its members to which they must adhere.

Four years later the Association adopted the 'Code of Athens', an international code of ethics for public relations, as its moral charter. The Code is based upon the principles of the UN Universal Declaration of Human Rights. See Appendix I.

The Association received formal recognition by the United Nations in 1964 on a consultative basis to the Economic and Social Council. It has now also received recognition by Unesco as a non-governmental organisation in the 'mutual information category of relationship'.

Membership of IPRA is open only to those who have been in public relations practice at a senior level for at least five years and are of known professional competence. All members are elected in their personal capacity and with over 800 members in 65 different countries IPRA comprises a unique international network of professional competence and experience in public relations and related fields. While IPRA remains a body of individual practitioners, it works closely with national public relations associations and regional federations.

Further information is available from: International Public Relations Association, Case Postale 126, CH-1211 Geneva 20, Switzerland.

Index